# CityPack
## *Prague*

**MICHAEL IVORY**

*Michael Ivory's passion for Prague is a long-standing one. He is both a landscape architect and freelance travel writer, and lectures on the city and revisits it whenever possible. His books for the AA include* Essential Hungary, Essential Czech Republic *and* Explorer Prague.

City-centre map continues on inside back cover

AA Publishing

# Contents

# About this book

## KEY TO SYMBOLS

✚ map reference on the fold-out map accompanying this book (see below)

✉ address

☎ telephone number

🕐 opening times

🍴 restaurant or café on premises or near by

🚇 nearest underground train station

🚆 nearest overground train station

🚌 nearest bus route

⛴ nearest riverboat or ferry stop

♿ facilities for visitors with disabilities

✋ admission charge

↔ other nearby places of interest

❓ tours, lectures or special events

▶ cross-reference (see below)

ℹ tourist information

## ORGANISATION

CityPack Prague's six sections cover the six most important aspects of your visit to Prague:

- Prague life – the city and its people
- Itineraries, walks and excursions – how to organise your time
- The top 25 sights, arranged from west to east across the city
- Features about different aspects of the city that make it special
- Detailed listings of hotels, restaurants, shops and nightlife
- Practical information

In addition, text boxes provide fascinating extra facts and snippets, highlights of places to visit and invaluable practical advice.

## CROSS-REFERENCES

To help you make the most of your visit, cross-references, indicated by ▶ , show you where to find additional information about a place or subject.

## MAPS

- The fold-out map in the wallet at the back of the book is a comprehensive street plan of Prague. All the map references given in the book refer to this map. For example, the National Theatre on Národní 2, Nové město has the following information: ✚ D/E5 – indicating the grid squares of the map in which the National Theatre will be found.

- The city-centre maps found on the inside front and back covers of the book itself are for quick reference. They show the Top 25 Sights, described on pages 24–48, which are clearly plotted by number ( ❶ – ㉕, not page number) from west to east.

## PRICES

Where appropriate, an indication of the cost of an establishment is given by £ signs: £££ denotes higher prices, ££ denotes average prices, while £ denotes lower charges.

# PRAGUE
*life*

# Introducing Prague

*St Nicholas's Church,
seen from Hradčany*

'Golden Prague', 'Prague the hundred-towered', 'the most beautiful city in Europe': such clichés are certainly true, though they tell only part of the story. Ochre in colour, many of the city's buildings do gleam like gold, especially in the glow of the late afternoon sun; the skyline is indeed punctuated by uncountable towers, turrets, and steeples; and Prague's beauty is incontestable.

The site is superb, with rock bluffs above a broad and curving river, and steep slopes rising through orchards and woodland. Human activities have enhanced what Nature provided so generously, crowning the heights with great churches and palaces, emphasising the slopes with terraced gardens, precipitous streets and flights of stairs, and marking the course of the river with a sequence of foaming weirs and bold bridges.

Over a thousand years of history is expressed in stone: the foundations of the first Christian churches can still be seen, while below the pavements of the Old Town are vaulted cellars that once formed the ground floor of medieval merchants' houses. In the 17th and 18th centuries the baroque style transformed the city's appearance. In the 19th century came great landmarks such as the National Museum and National Theatre – testimony to the Czech nation's self-confidence – followed by the extravagances of art nouveau. Even the radical architects of the first half of the 20th century managed to insert their innovative buildings into the urban scene with a minimum of disturbance.

### Urban decay

Visitors are sometimes shocked at the shabby state of some of Prague's buildings. Under Communism, showpieces were restored at great public expense, but less favoured buildings mouldered away, encased in strait-jackets of scaffolding to stop them falling into the street. But privatisation and restitution (the return of property to its former owners) has gone far to remedy the situation.

In spite of (or perhaps as a result of?) military defeats, occupation and denial of citizens' rights, the four distinct quarters that form Prague's historic core are in a near-perfect state of preservation. They are: the Castle district (Hradčany), the Lesser Town (Malá Strana) at its foot, the Old Town (Staré město) across the river, and the New Town (Nové město) laid out in the 14th century.

Beyond is a ring of run-down suburbs, largely 19th-century, then an outer circle of high-rise estates and satellite towns built during the last 40 years. These suburbs are where most Praguers live. For many, life after Communism remains grey, the struggle to make ends meet greater than ever. Others have embraced the new freedom with alacrity; there's an obvious enjoyment in the previously forbidden pleasures of making and spending money. The continuing stream of visitors from abroad adds an extra element of vibrancy and has vastly improved the places to eat and to stay. Entrepreneurs are everywhere, opening shops, cafés and bars. There's excitement in the air, particularly among the young, as Prague claims its rightful place in a Europe from which it has long been excluded.

### Get lost

Prague is a labyrinth, a warren of winding roads and alleyways, courtyards and passageways leading deep into buildings. Don't mind getting lost – treat disorientation as a pleasure and enjoy the unexpected treats along the way. The historic centre is small, and sooner or later you will recognise a landmark or emerge by the riverside.

*Míseňská Street, Malá Strana*

# PRAGUE IN FIGURES

**GEOGRAPHY**
- Prague, located in Central Europe and situated on the River Vltava, is the capital of the Czech Republic (and was until 1993 the capital of Czechoslovakia)
- Prague lies 50°5' north and 14°25' east
- Area: 497 sq km
- Lowest point (River Vltava): 176m above sea-level
- Highest point (Kopanina): 396m above sea-level
- Distance from Berlin: 350km
- Distance from Vienna: 292km
- Distance from Paris: 1,037km
- Distance from London: 1,377km

**PEOPLE**
- Population: 1,225,000; 95.5 per cent are of Czech nationality
- Living conditions: about half the population lives in *paneláks*, the high-rise flats built under Communism. The largest housing estate is 'Southwest Town', with a planned population that should reach a total of 140,000 inhabitants
- Nearly half of Prague's population leaves the city on summer weekends, many to spend time in their *chata*, or country cottage
- 43,000 students attend universities in the city

**ENVIRONMENT**
- Conservation: the city's historic core, designated by Unesco as being of world importance, covers an area of 900 hectares and includes some 10,000 protected artefacts and works of art
- The city has nearly 10,000 hectares of green spaces (parks, cemeteries etc)
- Nearly 750,000 vehicles fill the 2,800km of city streets. Prague's Metro, 44km long and with 46 stations, carries more than a third of all the city's public transport passengers. There are 136km of tram lines within the city
- Prague is a heavily polluted city. Its industries, heating plants and motor vehicles emit more than 30,000 tonnes of sulphur dioxide per annum

# PRAGUE PEOPLE

### VÁCLAV HAVEL

Playwright and one-time prominent dissident President Havel, by attempting to combine political activity with ethical principles, has not always endeared himself to market-obsessed politicians keen to rush the new republic into the embrace of modern capitalism. Gruff of voice and short of stature, Havel has survived ill-treatment by secret police and a chain-smoking past, but his shaky state of health is a cause for concern among many citizens, who see him as an irreplaceable asset to this fledgling democracy.

### IVAN PLICKA

Engineer Plicka has spent most of his working life in the section of the City Architect's Department responsible for the planning of Greater Prague. Now near retirement, he is proud of the city's beauty and of his office's role in preserving it. He hopes his department's forth-

*Engineer Ivan Plicka*

coming masterplan to take Prague into the next millennium will protect the city centre from the commercial pressures that have destroyed the traditional character of many a Western city.

### LENKA CHOBOTOVÁ

Lively Lenka, one of a generation of young people who experienced Communism only as small children, graduated from a high school specialising in information sciences. A six-month stay in the UK gave her fluency in English, and she hopes to study English literature at one of Prague's universities, although for the time being she is happy to earn a modest living as a librarian. Cheerful and outgoing, Lenka has a zest for life that expresses itself in getting together with like-minded friends to sing and make music in one of the city's innumerable pubs.

**Jo Williams**

Art historian Jo hails from New York city and is one of a number of young Americans who have been attracted to post-Communist Prague. An enthusiast for Czech culture, she has not only mastered the language but works in a Czech environment at a local salary, helping to raise the profile of an arts foundation. Her first job was to promote abroad the hidden treasures of the National Gallery's modern art collection in the Veletržní palác.

# A CHRONOLOGY

| | |
|---|---|
| **7th or 8th century AD** | Prague's legendary foundation by Princess Libuše and her ploughman husband, Přemysl |
| **Late 9th century** | A Slav stronghold is established on Hradčany Hill, where Prince Bořivoj builds the first timber church |
| **10th century** | Trading settlements are established in Lesser Town (Malá Strana) and Old Town (Staré město) |
| **1231** | King Wenceslas I fortifies the Old Town with 13 towers, 12m-high walls and a moat (today's Na příkopě, or Moat Street) |
| **1253–78** | Reign of King Otakar II, who extends and fortifies Malá Strana, inviting German merchants and traders to settle there |
| **1346–78** | Under King/Emperor Charles IV, St Vitus's Cathedral is begun, the New Town (Nové město) is laid out and Charles Bridge is built |
| **1415** | Religious reformer Jan Hus is burnt at the stake for heresy |
| **1576–1611** | Reign of eccentric Emperor Rudolph II |
| **1620** | Battle of the White Mountain just outside Prague, in which the Protestant army is routed. In the following years, Protestant leaders are executed in Old Town Square. Czechs who refuse to reconvert to Catholicism emigrate *en masse*. A largely foreign nobility is installed, loyal to the Habsburgs, and Prague is beautified with baroque churches and palaces. The Court makes Vienna its principal seat and Prague becomes a sleepy provincial town |
| **1848** | A revolt led by students is put down by Austrian General Windischgrätz, but Czech nationalism continues to grow |
| **1914–18** | Czechs are dragged into World War I on the Austrian side. Many soldiers desert or join the Czech Legion fighting for the Allies in Russia, Italy and France |

**1918** Establishment of the democratic First Republic of Czechoslovakia under liberal President Tomáš Masaryk

**1938** Britain and France agree to cede the Sudeten-land to Hitler's Germany, depriving Czechoslovakia of most of its industry and all its defences

**1939** Hitler dismembers what is left of Czechoslovakia. The Czech Lands become the 'Protectorate of Bohemia-Moravia', and Prague is declared the 'Fourth City of the Third Reich'

**1942** The assassination of Reichsprotektor Heydrich by Czechoslovak parachutists flown in from Britain leads to brutal repression by the Nazis

**1945** The people of Prague liberate their city and welcome in the Red Army. Over 2.5 million Germans are expelled from the Sudetenland

**1948** Communists, the most powerful party in the democratically elected government, stage a *coup d'état*. Stalinist repression follows

**1968** The Prague Spring, an attempt to change Communism into 'Socialism with a human face', is crushed by Soviet tanks

**1977** Dissident intellectuals sign Charter 77, a call for the government to apply the Helsinki Agreements of 1975. Many, including Václav Havel, are harrassed and imprisoned on trumped-up charges

**1989** The Velvet Revolution. The Communist government resigns and is replaced by the dissident-led Civic Forum. Václav Havel is elected President

**1993** Czechoslovakia splits into the independent states of Slovakia and the Czech Republic (with Prague as the latter's capital)

**1997** The Czech economy stalls and the government falls amid corruption accusations

11

# PEOPLE & EVENTS FROM HISTORY

### Fall from power

Yet another Prague defenestration (not officially referred to as such) was the fall of much-loved foreign minister Jan Masaryk from his office window in the Černin Palace when the Communists seized power in 1948. His opposition to Communism led many to think that he was pushed, but it is more likely that he jumped, in despair at the prospect facing his country and at his powerlessness to prevent it.

## DEFENESTRATIONS

Prague's history was marked by several defenestrations – in which political opponents were violently ejected from upper-floor windows. The first, in 1419, seems to have happened spontaneously. A crowd of Hussites demonstrating in Charles Square was pelted with stones from the New Town Hall by their Catholic adversaries, who – to make matters worse – were German. The infuriated mob stormed the building and threw the culprits from the first-floor windows on to the cobbles of the square, where they were brutally killed. A window of the Old Town Hall provided the means for expressing discontent in 1483, when the mayor of Prague was the victim of the second defenestration.

The third defenestration, of 1618, marked the start of the Thirty Years War. A group of Protestant noblemen forced their way into Prague Castle and hurled a pair of Catholic councillors and their secretary into the dung-heaps that had accumulated in the moat. The victims' survival – the manure broke their fall – was widely attributed to divine intervention.

*Alexander Dubček*

## FALSE SPRING

By the mid-1960s, the oppressiveness of the Communist system in Czechoslovakia was becoming all too apparent. In what came to be known as the 'Prague Spring' of 1968, the Party under Alexander Dubček promised to create 'Socialism with a human face'. Terrified at this prospect, the Soviet Union sent in tanks in August and took the government off to Moscow in chains. A humiliated Dubček was first told to reverse his reforms, and then sacked. Two decades of social and political winter followed, ended by the Velvet Revolution in 1989.

# PRAGUE
## *how to organise your time*

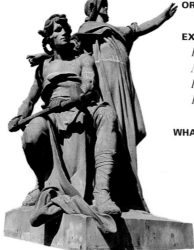

# ITINERARIES

These four itineraries, all beginning from the 'Golden Cross' – the pedestrianised area where Wenceslas Square (Václavské náměstí) meets Národní třída and Na příkopě – are based on Prague's four historic districts.

| | |
|---|---|
| **ITINERARY ONE** | OLD TOWN & JOSEFOV |
| **Morning** | Walk east along Na příkopě (Moat Street) Municipal House (➤ 46) Walk along Celetná Street to the Old Town Square (Staroměstské náměstí; ➤ 42) Coffee at one of the cafés in Old Town Square Climb the tower of the Old Town Hall Astronomical Clock (➤ 59) Take in Týn Church and Týn Court (➤ 55) Walk along Pařížská (Paris Boulevard) to the Old/New Synagogue (➤ 39) |
| **Lunch** | Restaurants on Pařížská |
| **Afternoon** | Old Jewish Cemetery (➤ 40) Decorative Arts Museum (➤ 37) |
| **ITINERARY TWO** | HRADČANY, THE CASTLE HILL |
| **Morning** | Go west along 28 října and Národní streets Catch Tram No 22 at the Národní třída stop (Bila Hora direction) to the Pohořelec stop Strahov Monastery (➤ 24) Coffee in Pohořelec Square Continue to the Loretto Shrine (➤ 26) Follow Černínska Street to Nový Svět (➤ 25) Prague Castle (➤ 29) |
| **Lunch** | One of the Castle restaurants |
| **Afternoon** | St Vitus's Cathedral (➤ 30) St George's Basilica and Convent (➤ 31) Head through Castle Gardens (➤ 58) and go via Nerudova (➤ 32) to Malá Strana Square Return to the Golden Cross by Tram No 22 or on foot across the Charles Bridge |
| **ITINERARY THREE** | OVER THE BRIDGE TO MALÁ STRANA |
| **Morning** | Enter the Old Town via Na můstku and Havelská ulička, turn left into the market held |

on Havelská and V kotcích streets, and
continue westwards via Uhelný trh and
Skořepka Street into Bethlehem Square
Bethlehem Chapel (➤ 55)
Náprstek Museum (➤ 53)
Coffee in café or restaurant on Bethlehem
Square
Follow Husova Street and turn left into the
Royal Way on Karlova Street
Cross Charles Bridge
Turn right into Josefská Street and again into
Letenská Street
Wallenstein Palace (➤ 34)

**Lunch**   Restaurant or café in Malá Strana Square

**Afternoon**   St Nicholas's Church (➤ 33)
Schönborn and Lobkovic Palaces (➤ 54)
Church of Our Lady Victorious (➤ 55)
Walk via Mostecká and Lázěnská to Maltese
Square and Grand Priors' Square with the John
Lennon Wall
Cross the Čertovka brook to Na kampě on
Kampa Island
Return via Legions' Bridge (Most legií) and
the National Theatre (➤ 36)

**ITINERARY FOUR**   NEW TOWN & VYŠEHRAD

**Morning**   Walk west into Jungmann Square
(Jungmannovo náměstí)
Stroll in the Franciscans' Garden
(Františkánská zahrada) behind the Church of
Our Lady of the Snows
Wenceslas Square (➤ 43); stop for coffee
National Museum (➤ 44)

**Lunch**   Restaurant or café in Wenceslas Square

**Afternoon**   Metro to Vyšehrad
Palace of Culture
Go west along Na Bučance and V pevnosti
Vyšehrad (➤ 38)
Tram No 3, then return to Wenceslas Square
via Vodičkova Street and Novák building
(U Novaku; ➤ 56)

# WALKS

## THE SIGHTS

- Old Town Hall (➤ 42)
- Clam-Gallas Palace
- Old Town Bridge Tower (➤ 35)
- Charles Bridge (➤ 35)
- St Nicholas's Church, Malá Strana (➤ 33)
- Neruda Street (➤ 32)

## INFORMATION

**Distance** 2km
**Time** 1 hour
**Start point** Old Town Square (Staroměstské náměstí)
➕ E4
Ⓢ Staroměstská
**End point** Hradčany Square (Hradčany náměstí)
➕ C4
🚊 Tram 22

## Surface restoration

With their often ambivalent attitude to tradition, the Communists decided to promote the Royal Way (see Walk) as a tourist route, restoring the buildings along it. But the treatment was sometimes more of a face-lift than a complete rejuvenation.

### IN THE FOOTSTEPS OF KINGS – THE OLD TOWN TO THE CASTLE

This walk follows the Royal Way, the ancient coronation route taken by Czech kings from their downtown residence to the Cathedral high up in Hradčany. It starts in Old Town Square, and is deservedly popular so you are likely to have plenty of company.

Go west into Little Square (Malé náměstí), with its delightful fountain, and turn into twisting Karlova Street, with its tempting gift shops. The street's final curve brings you into Knights of the Cross Square (Křížovnicke náměstí). Look out for the traffic as you rush to enjoy the incomparable view of the Castle across the river.

Pass through the Old Town Bridge Tower on to Charles Bridge; admire the stunning procession of saintly statues that adorn its parapets. As it approaches Malá Strana, the bridge becomes a flyover, and then, after the Malá Strana Bridge Tower, leads you to Mostecká (Bridge) Street. Malá Strana Square (Malostranské náměstí), dominated by the great bulk of St Nicholas's Church, needs crossing with care. Grit your teeth in preparation for the long climb up Nerudova (Neruda) Street, and don't forget to turn sharp right onto the final leg of the Castle approach, named Ke hradu. Regain your breath while leaning on the wall of Hradčany Square and soak up the panorama of the city far below, a just reward for the climb.

*Café in Old Town Square*

*Ceiling in the Schwarzenberg Palace*

## THE SIGHTS

- Schwarzenberg Palace (Military Museum; ➤ 53)
- Strahov Monastery (➤ 24)
- Černin Palace (➤ 54)
- Loretto Shrine (➤ 26)
- Nový Svět (➤ 25)
- Šternberg Palace (➤ 27)
- Archbishop's Palace (➤ 54)
- Royal Gardens (➤ 58)
- Letná Plain (➤ 50)
- Josefov, the Ghetto (➤ 39, 40)

## INFORMATION

**Distance** 4km
**Time** 2 hours
**Start point** Hradčany Square (Hradčany náměstí)
🔲 C4
🚋 Tram 22
**End point** Old Town Square (Staroměstské náměstí)
🔲 E4
Ⓜ Staroměstská

## BACK TO THE OLD TOWN VIA SOME OF PRAGUE'S GARDENS

From Hradčany Square walk up Loretánská Street, turning 180 degrees left as you enter Pohořelec Square. A short way down Úvoz, turn sharp right and stop to enjoy the view from the vineyard lying just below Strahov Monastery. Go through the monastery courtyard, turning right into Pohořelec, then left into Loretto Square (Loretánské náměstí). Narrow Černinská Street leads downhill into Nový Svět.

Return to Hradčany Square via Nový Svět and Kanovnická. Go through the Matthias Gate of the Castle, then out of the north gate from the Castle's Second Courtyard. Turn into the Royal Gardens; leave them near the Belvedere summer palace and enter the Chotek Gardens (Chotkovy sady). Cross the footbridge into Letná Plain (Letenské sady), and view the city first from the Hanava Pavilion (Hanavský pavilon) and then from the plinth where Stalin's statue stood. Descend the steps and ramps to the Čech Bridge (Čechův most) and return to Old Town Square via Josefov – the former Jewish ghetto.

### Rustic retreat

The tiny vineyard below Strahov Monastery is a remnant from the days when vines clad the slopes hereabouts. Young apple, pear, cherry and almond trees have been planted, giving a landscape unique in the heart of a metropolitan city.

17

# EVENING STROLLS

## INFORMATION

**The Old Town**
**Distance** 1.5km
**Time** 1 hour
**Start point** National Museum
(Návodní Muzeum)
⊞ F5
🚇 Muzeum
**End point** Smetana statue
⊞ D4
🚇 Staroměstská

## THE OLD TOWN

Survey the busy city centre scene from the terrace in front of the National Museum at the top of Wenceslas Square before leaving through the underpass (don't try to cross the road) and walk down either side of the Square, having first ensured that your wallet or handbag is safe. Keep going in the same direction at the foot of the Square, along Na můstku and Melantrichova into Old Town Square. Follow the Royal Way (► 16), turning left into Husova Street, then right into Bethlehem Square (Betlémské náměstí), a quieter focus of night-life. Head down Náprstkova Street and join the Vltava embankment, crossing the road carefully. The best point to absorb the view of the river, Malá Strana and the Castle is from the tip of Novotného lávka, by the statue of Smetana.

*View over Malá Strana*

## INFORMATION

**The New Town**
**Distance** 3km
**Time** 1½ hours
**Start and end point**
Smetana statue
⊞ D4
🚇 Staroměstská

## THE NEW TOWN

Finish your beer or coffee in one of the cafés by the Smetana statue and go through the arcade leading to Knights of the Cross Square at the Old Town end of Charles Bridge. Continue in the same direction, then cross the Vltava by the restored Mánes Bridge (Mánesův most). Head for Malostranská Metro station and walk through what is probably the only underground railway garden in the world to palace-lined Valdštejnská Street, with its unusual close-up view of the Castle high above. Tomášská Street leads into Malá Strana Square. Return to the Smetana statue down Mostecká Street and across Charles Bridge, which is particularly enchanting at night.

# Organised Tours

There are plenty of general tours of the city, as well as more detailed explorations of particular districts and trips that venture out into the surroundings. The difficulty lies in choosing between them, but the best advice is to shop around and consider all the alternatives on offer.

## PIS

A good starting point for finding out about organised tours is the official Prague Information Service (Pražská informační služba – PIS), at: ✉ Na příkopě 20, Nové město ☎ 54 44 44 or 187 🕐 Winter Mon–Fri 9–6; Sat 9–3. Summer Mon–Fri 9–7; Sat–Sun 9–5 Ⓜ Náměsti Republiky; or ✉ Můstek or Staroměstské náměsti 1 (Old Town Hall) ☎ 54 44 44 or 187 🕐 Winter Mon–Fri 9–6; Sat–Sun 9–5. Summer Mon–Fri 9–7; Sat–Sun 9–6 Ⓜ Staroměstská or Můstek. PIS also runs its own tours in a reliable way.

## MAIN TOUR OPERATORS

Čedok (the longest-established travel company of all) at: ✉ Na příkopě 18, Nové město ☎ 2419 7111; fax 2422 3479 Ⓜ Náměsti Republiky or Můstek; ✉ Pařížská 6, Staré město ☎ 231 6978; fax 232 17 28 Ⓜ Staroměstská; and ✉ Rytířská 16, Staré město ☎ 26 36 97; fax 26 27 96 Ⓜ Můstek or Staroměstská.

Premiant City Tour is at: ✉ Na příkopě 23, Nové město ☎ 0601 21 26 25 (mobile).

## WALKING TOURS

A main starting point for themed walks in the historic city centre is Old Town Square; check local posters for starting times. Also Prague Walks ✉ Václavské náměsti 60 ☎ 61 21 46 03.

## BOAT TOURS

Boat tours along the Vltava range from short trips, an hour or so in length, to long excursions that include lunch or dinner.
EVD 🚩 E3 ✉ Quayside at Na Františku (near the southern end of Čechův most) ☎ 23 10 208/23 11 915 Ⓜ Staroměstská.
PPS 🚩 D5 ✉ Rašinova nábřeži (south of Jiráskův most) ☎ 29 38 09/29 83 09 Ⓜ Karlovo náměsti.

### Castle tour

A stroll around the Castle in the company of a well-informed guide can be instructive. Tours start from the Third Courtyard (🚩 C4 ✉ Hradčany ☎ 2437 3368).

*View across the Vltava river to Prague Castle*

# EXCURSIONS

*Karlštejn Castle*

## KARLŠTEJN CASTLE (HRAD KARLŠTEJN)

This mighty fortress, one of the great sights of Bohemia, towers above the glorious woodlands of the gorge of the River Berounka. There's no motor transport up from the riverside village, but the superb panorama from the castle walls will fully compensate you for the long climb up. The name of the castle, which was started in 1348, celebrates the emperor Charles IV. He conceived it as a sort of sacred bunker, a repository for the Crown Jewels and his collection of holy relics. Not merely a fortress, the castle was also planned as a personal, processional way which the emperor would follow to its climax – the Great Tower containing the Chapel of the Holy Rood, reached only after much prayer and contemplation. This gorgeous chamber has had to be sealed off from the public, whose breath was destroying its exquisite artefacts.

## INFORMATION

**Karlštejn Castle**

✉ Hrad Karlštejn

☎ 0311 68 46 17

🕔 Jan–Mar, Nov–Dec Tue–Sun
9–12, 1–4. Apr, Oct
Tue–Sun 9–12, 1–5.
May–Jun, Sep Tue–Sun
9–12, 12:30–6. Jul–Aug
Tue–Sun 9–12, 12:30–7

🚆 Suburban trains from
Prague-Smíchov to Karlštejn:
journey time 40 mins

**Mělník Castle**

✉ Svatováclavská, Mělník

☎ 0206 62 21 21

🕔 Mar–Dec daily 10–5

🚌 Bus from Florenc coach
station: journey time 50
mins

## MĚLNÍK

Built on a bluff near the confluence of the Vltava and Elbe rivers, this ancient town is famous for the vineyards that rise up in terraces beneath its imposing castle. Following the demise of Communism, Mělník's castle and estates have been returned to the original aristocratic Lobkovic owners. Long before the Lobkovic family, however, it was a royal seat, the abode of the Czech queens, one of whom raised her grandson Wenceslas (later the 'Good King') here. The castle courtyard, with its Gothic and Renaissance wings and ancient wine-cellars, is approached via the charmingly arcaded town square.

## LIDICE

Nowhere could seem more ordinary than this modern little mining village in the dull countryside just beyond Prague airport. But on 10 June 1942, on the flimsiest of pretexts, its male population was shot and its women and children

*St Peter and St Paul Church, Mělník Castle*

sent off to a concentration camp – and Lidice's name resounded round the world as a synonym for Czech suffering and German ruthlessness. Days before, Reichsprotektor Heydrich had been assassinated, and the Nazis needed revenge. Lidice was razed to the ground and its name removed from the records 'forever'. After the war the village was rebuilt a short distance away, while the site of the atrocity became a memorial museum and park.

## KONOPIŠTĚ CASTLE (ZÁMEK KONOPIŠTĚ)

Konopiště Castle's round towers rise in romantic fashion above the surrounding woodlands. The palace's origins go back to the 14th century, but it owes its present appearance largely to Archduke Franz Ferdinand, heir to the Habsburg throne, who acquired it in 1887. The corridors are filled with trophies of the countless wild creatures he slaughtered while waiting for the demise of his long-lived uncle Franz Josef. The archduke met his own violent end when he was cut down by an assassin's bullet in Sarajevo, thereby triggering the start of World War I. The castle is full of Franz Ferdinand's fine furniture and his extraordinary collection of weapons. His other obsession was landscape gardening, and the splendid parklands and rose garden are a delight.

## INFORMATION

**Lidice**
- ✉ Monument: 10 cervna 1942, Lidice
- ☎ 0312 92 33 52
- 🕐 Jan–Mar, Nov–Dec daily 9–3. Apr–Oct daily 8–5
- 🚌 Bus from Dejvická Metro stop

**Konopiště Castle**
- ✉ Zámek Konopiště, Benesov u Prahy
- ☎ 0301 213 66
- 🕐 Apr, Oct Tue–Sun 9–12, 1–3. May–Aug Tue–Sun 9–12, 1–5. Sep Tue–Sun 9–12, 1–4
- 🚂 Train to Benesov (1 hr) then bus or taxi

# WHAT'S ON

**MAY/JUNE**  *Prague Spring Music Festival* (mid-May): this internationally important event consists of an array of concerts of classical music in churches, palaces and halls. It starts off with a procession from Smetana's grave in the National Cemetery in Vyšehrad to the great hall named after him in the recently restored Obecni dům (Municipal House), where a rousing performance of his orchestral tone poem *Ma Vlast* ('*My Country*') is given

**JUNE**  *Dance Prague*: an international dance festival with events at various venues, including some public outdoor spaces

**OCTOBER**  *Mozart Festival*: the cultural programme for the month includes even more than the usual Prague allowance of the maestro's masterworks

**DECEMBER**  *St Nicholas* (5 December): the streets are roamed by a multitude of St Nicks, each accompanied by an angel (who rewards good children with sweets) and a devil (who chastises appropriately)

*Christmas Eve* (24 December): live carp are sold on the streets for the traditional Czech Christmas Eve dinner

*New Year's Eve* (31 December): those wanting to celebrate formally attend 'Sylvester' balls, while others welcome the arrival of the New Year on the streets

## TICKETS
Tickets for events can be obtained at individual box offices (which may be cheaper) or through one of a number of agencies. These include:

Prague Information Service ✉ Na příkope 20, Nové město ☎ 26 40 20 or ✉ Old Town Hall ☎ 24 48 20 18.

Ticketpro ✉ Salvátorská 10, Staré město ☎ 24 81 40 20.

## ENTERTAINMENT INFORMATION
The best source of information for English-readers about what's on is probably the tabloid section 'Night and Day' of the weekly newspaper *Prague Post*. This gives listings of stage, screen and cultural events likely to be relevant to visitors from abroad, as well as interesting comment and analysis. A comprehensive review of forthcoming events is contained in *Cultural Events*, published monthly by the Prague Information Service.

# PRAGUE's
## *top 25 sights*

*The sights are shown on the maps on the inside front cover and inside back cover, numbered* **1–25** *from west to east across the city*

# STRAHOV MONASTERY

## HIGHLIGHTS

- 17th-century Theological Hall
- 18th-century Philosophical Hall
- Strahov Picture Galley (Strahovská obrazárna)
- 9th-century Strahov Gospels
- Interior of Church of the Assumption

## INFORMATION

- C4
- Strahovské nádvoří 1, Hradčany
- 2051 6671
- Daily 9–12, 1–5
- Peklo (Hell) restaurant in monastery cellars
- Tram 22 to Pohořelec
- Fair
- Moderate
- Loretto Shrine (➤ 26), Petřín Hill (➤ 28)

*Baroque spires rising towards Heaven, a gilded image of an enemy of the Faith, monks profiting from an enterprise in Hell: this hilltop monastery (Strahovský klášter) seems to encapsulate something of this most paradoxical of cities.*

**Persuasive priests** The Strahov Monastery, a major landmark in the cityscape, crowns the steep slope leading up from Malá Strana (its name derives from *strahovní*, meaning 'to watch over'). It is a treasure house of literature, and its ornate library halls with their splendid frescos are among the most magnificent in Europe. As befits a monastery devoted to books, Strahov owed much to its abbots' way with words. Its 12th-century founder, Abbot Zdík, persuaded Prince Vladislav II to back his project by making flattering comparisons of Prague with the holy city of Jerusalem. Much later, in 1783, Abbot Meyer exercised equal powers of persuasion on Emperor Joseph II to exempt Strahov from the reforming ruler's edict which closed down many of the Habsburg Empire's monasteries. Such was the eloquence of the canny cleric that Strahov actually benefited from the misfortune of other institutions: books from the suppressed monastery at Louka were brought here by the wagonload. A gilded medallion of the emperor over the library entrance may also have helped to persuade Joseph that the Strahov monks deserved special treatment.

**Returnees' revenge** The monks, who belong to the Premonstratensian Order, were chased out of Strahov by the Communists in 1952 but have now come back. They have made the upper floor of the cloisters into a gallery for the works of art since returned to them, and converted the cellars into a restaurant called Hell (Peklo).

# NOVÝ SVĚT

*Skivvies and scullions, footmen and flunkies, these were the folk for whom the humble homes of Nový Svět ('New World') were originally erected back in the 14th century. The area is now more up-market.*

**Wizards and weird doings** Nový Svět, a mysterious place of crooked alleyways and secret gardens hidden behind high walls, has never been in the city's mainstream. Aside from the Castle servants, those able to cater for the more esoteric interests of their masters came here. They included the Danish astronomer Tycho Brahe and his German colleague Johannes Kepler, both employed by Rudolph II to investigate the more arcane secrets of the universe.

**La Bohème** Today's residents are artists and writers, who have colonised the pretty 18th-century houses along this charming cobbled street, wobbling its way westwards just uphill from the Castle. The painter's studio at No 19 is crammed with pictures of curvaceous girls and grimacing gnomes, while the Czech master of animated film, Jan Švankmajer, a long-time resident, runs a gallery devoted to Surrealist art.

**Connecting the worlds** 'New World' is linked to the outside world by short streets (Loretánská, Kapucínská, U Kasáren and Kanovnická) that run down the hill from the main tourist trail between the Strahov Monastery and the Castle, or by flights of steps that lead from the old ramparts (whose course is followed by today's tram No 22).

## HIGHLIGHTS

- Nepomuk statue in Černinská Street
- Birthplace of violinist F Ondříček at No 25
- Tycho Brahe's house at No 1
- Church of St John Nepomuk
- No 3, the President's favourite restaurant

## INFORMATION

- ✚ C4
- ✉ Nový Svět, Hradčany
- 🍴 Restaurant at No 3
- 🚊 Tram 22 to Brusnice
- ♿ Few
- ↔ Loretto Shrine (▶ 26)

*St John Nepomuk*

**3**

# LORETTO SHRINE

- The main façade, with statuary and carillon
- The Santa Casa
- Interior of the Church of the Nativity
- Diamond monstrance in the Loretto Treasure
- Cloister painting of St Starosta

*Loretto Shrine, Hradčany*

## INFORMATION

- ⊞ C4
- ✉ Loretánské náměstí, Hradčany
- ☎ 2051 6740
- ⏱ Tue–Sun 9–12:15, 1–4:30
- 🚋 Tram 22 to Pohořelec
- ♿ None
- 💰 Moderate
- ↔ Strahov Monastery (➤ 24), Nový Svět (➤ 25)

*A bearded lady, skeletons rattling their bones to the sound of chiming bells, severed breasts on display, a flying house... these are not part of a freak show, but instead are all features of the sumptuous Loretto Shrine (Loreta), high up on Hradčany Hill.*

**Counter-Reformation fireworks** No showman's trick was spared to bring the wayward Czechs back into the Catholic fold after their long flirtation with Protestantism had been brought to an end by the Battle of the White Mountain in 1620. Protestant austerity, with its dislike of images, was replaced by the idolatry of the cult of the Virgin Mary, dripping with sensuality and symbolism. Of all the flights of architectural fantasy that the Roman Catholic Counter-Reformation perpetrated on Prague, the Loretto is the most bizarre as well as the most beautiful, its church and courtyard a theatre of cults, miracles and mysteries designed to dazzle doubters and sceptics.

**Weird wonders** The kernel of the complex is a Santa Casa, a facsimile of the Virgin Mary's holy home in Nazareth, supposedly flown by angels from the Holy Land and deposited at Loreta in Italy. Fifty such shrines were once scattered around the Czech countryside, but this is far and away the most important, an ornate little Renaissance pavilion built in 1631 and later given an equally ornate baroque setting of courtyard, carillon tower and richly decorated church. Pilgrims once flocked here in huge numbers to marvel at the macabre: St Agatha offering up her bloody bosom to the angels; the skeletons in their wax death masks; unhappy St Starosta, whose father killed her in a fury on finding she'd grown a beard to discourage a favoured suitor...

# ŠTERNBERG PALACE

*Who would guess that the unpretentious little alley beside the Prague Archbishop's palace on Hradčany Square would lead to one of the Continent's great art collections? Housed in the Šternberg Palace (Šternberský palác), it dazzles visitors with its Old Masters and modern works.*

**Ambitious aristocrats** Having built the Troja Château (▶ 48) on the edge of Prague, Count Šternberg, one of the city's richest men, needed a town house closer to Prague Castle. The Italian architect Giovanni Alliprandi was commissioned to design the palace, and work began on the count's Hradčany home in 1698. However, the money ran out before the main façade (the principal purpose of which was to upstage his neighbour, the Archbishop) could be completed. The interior was decorated with fine ceiling and wall paintings. It was a later Šternberg who donated much of the family's great picture collection to the fledgling National Gallery in the early 19th century, and the nation's finest foreign paintings were housed here from 1814 to 1871. They are once more in this grand setting.

**Picture palace** Despite being tucked away behind Hradčany Square, the Šternberg Palace is an edifice of some substance, arranged around an imposing courtyard, with grand stairways and an oval pavilion facing the garden. The National Gallery of European Art attracts a stream of tourists – as well as art thieves, tempted (until it was tightened up not long ago) by laughably lax security. The pictures could keep an art lover busy for a whole day, though 'restitution' has returned some star exhibits to the owners from whom they were confiscated by the Communists.

## HIGHLIGHTS

- Triptych of the *Adoration of the Magi*, Giertgen tot Sint Jans
- *Adam and Eve*, Cranach
- *Feast of the Rosary*, Dürer
- *Scholar in his Study*, Rembrandt
- *Head of Christ*, El Greco
- Icons from 2nd-century Egypt
- *Beheading of St Dorothy*, Hans Baldung Grien
- *Martyrdom of St Florian*, Altdorfer
- *St Jerome*, Ribera
- *The Thames*, Canaletto

## INFORMATION

- ✠ C4
- ✉ Hradčanské náměstí 15, Hradčany
- ☎ 2051 4595
- ⏰ Tue–Sun 10–6
- 🚊 Tram 22 to Pražský hrad
- ♿ Few
- 💲 Moderate
- ↔ Military Museum, Schwarzenberg Palace (▶ 53), Prague Castle (▶ 29)

*Top:* Melancholie II, *Jan Zrzavý*

**5**

# PETŘÍN HILL

## HIGHLIGHTS

- Rozhledna – viewing tower
- 14th-century Hunger Wall
- Mirror Maze (Bludiště)
- Charles Bridge Battle diorama
- Observatory and Planetarium
- Rose Garden
- Alpine Garden
- Baroque Church of St Lawrence
- Calvary Chapel and Stations of the Cross
- Ukrainian timber Church of St Michael

## INFORMATION

- ➕ C–D4–5
- 🕐 Rozhledna: Apr–Aug daily 10–7. Sep–Oct daily 10–6. Nov–Mar Sat–Sun 10–5. Mirror Maze: Apr–Aug daily 10–7. Sep–Nov Mon–Fri 10–5; Sat–Sun 10–6. Nov–Mar Sat–Sun 10–5. Observatory: hours vary; for information call PIS on ☎ 54 44 44 or 187
- 🍽 Café and restaurant
- 🚊 Tram 22 to Strahov then walk
- 🚋 Funicular railway, Újezd in Malá Strana
- ♿ Few
- 🎟 Rozhledna, Mirror Maze, Observatory: moderate
- ↔ Strahov Monastery (▶ 24)

*When the press of the crowd on Charles Bridge becomes too much and the pavements become too hard, you can always retire to the glorious green of the Petřín. Its orchards and woodlands are a cool retreat from the pressures of the city centre.*

**A train with a view** In 1891 the thoughtful city fathers provided a jolly little funicular railway (the 'Lanovka') to the top of Petřín Hill. Now restored, it once again carries passengers effortlessly up (or down) the steep slope. At the top there's a whole array of attractions, including the little brother of the Eiffel Tower, called the Rozhledna ('Lookout'). This, too, was built in 1891, for the city's great Jubilee Expo which celebrated the achievements of the Czech provinces when they still formed part of the Austrian Empire. The tower's 299 steps lead to a viewing platform; some claim to have seen, on a clear day, not only the Czech Republic's Giant Mountains (150km to the north-east) but also the Alps (even further away to the south-west). And all of Prague lies at your feet.

**Country matters** With its woods and orchards (splendid with blossom in spring), the Petřín brings a real breath of the countryside into the metropolis and provides a counterpoint to the busy Castle area. Once there were vineyards on

the hill, but these didn't survive the Thirty Years War, and in the end were replaced by the superb gardens that link the palaces of Malá Strana to the surrounding hillside parklands.

# PRAGUE CASTLE

*The thousand windows of Prague Castle (Pražský hrad) gaze down into every corner of the city. This is the citadel of the Czech nation, the holder of its collective memory. It is a place of palaces, churches, streets, squares and alleyways, a city within a city, and the home of some of the country's greatest treasures.*

**Age-old stronghold** The princes of Prague first built a fortress on the limestone spur high above the Vltava in the 9th century, and the Czech Lands have been ruled from here ever since (except when rulers preferred to live in a long-vanished palace downtown or on the summit of the rock upstream at Vyšehrad). Every age has left its imprint on the Castle; it is a storehouse of architectural styles, ranging from the foundations of Romanesque churches a thousand years old to Professor Plečnik's premature Post-modernism of the interwar years. Even now, a committee is hard at work adapting the ancient complex in an attempt to make it more inviting and accessible to the citizens of a new and democratic order.

**Castle denizens** Teeming with tourists, the Castle's courtyards also echo to the tread of countless ghosts: Emperor Charles IV, with his dreams of Prague as a great imperial capital; the cranky Habsburg ruler Rudolph II, attended by his retinue of alchemists and necromancers, soothsayers and erotic painters; the Protestant mob that flung the hated Catholic councillors down from the Chancellery windows; Tomáš Masaryk, the philosopher-president who created Czechoslavakia; Adolf Hitler *Heil*-ing his hysterical helots; and, most recently, the Communists enjoying their privileges while they lasted.

## HIGHLIGHTS

- Giants guarding western gateway
- Mihulka (Powder Tower)
- Vladislav Hall in Old Royal Palace
- Tiny houses in Golden Lane
- Lobkovic Palace (History Museum)
- Outline of Matthias Gate in First Courtyard
- Second Courtyard, with Holy Rood Chapel
- Third Courtyard, with statue of St George
- Plečnik's canopy and stairway to gardens
- Riders' Staircase in Old Royal Palace

## INFORMATION

- C–D4
- Pražský hrad, Hradčany
- 2437 3368
- Courtyards and streets: daily until late. Buildings: Apr–Oct Tue–Sun 9–5. Nov–Mar Tue–Sun 9–4
- Cafés and restaurants
- Tram 22 to Pražský hrad
- Few
- Moderate
- Šternberg Palace (▶ 27), St Vitus's Cathedral (▶ 30)

# St Vitus's Cathedral

## HIGHLIGHTS

- South Portal, with 14th-century mosaic
- St Wenceslas's Chapel
- Crypt, with royal tombs
- Silver tomb of St John Nepomuk
- West front sculptures

## INFORMATION

- C/D4
- Pražský hrad, Hradčany
- Apr–Oct daily 9–5. Nov–Mar daily 9–4. Tower: Apr–Oct daily 10–5
- Restaurants and cafés in Castle
- Tram 22 to Pražský hrad
- Few
- Prague Castle (► 29)

*Tomb of St John Nepomuk*

*To emerge into Prague Castle's Third Courtyard and catch sight of the twin towers of St Vitus's Cathedral (katedrála svatého Víta) is a breathtaking experience, all the more compelling when you realise that the great Gothic edifice was completed only within living memory.*

**Spanning the centuries** The Cathedral was begun by Emperor Charles IV in the middle of the 14th century. It is built over the foundations of much earlier predecessors: a round church erected by 'Good King' Wenceslas in the early 10th century and a big Romanesque building resembling the present-day St George's Basilica (► 31). The glory of the architecture is largely due to the great Swabian builder Petr Parléř and his sons, who worked on the building for some 60 years. Progress was halted abruptly by the troubles of the 15th century, and the Cathedral consisted only of an east end until the formation of an 'Association for the Completion of the Cathedral', in 1843. Decades of effort saw the nave, western towers and much else brought to a triumphant conclusion; in 1929, a thousand years after King Wenceslas was assassinated, the cathedral was consecrated, dedicated to the country's patron saint, St Vitus.

**Cathedral treasures** The Cathedral is a treasure house of Bohemian history, though the Crown Jewels, its greatest prize, are seldom on display. The spacious interior absorbs the crowds with ease, and provides a fitting context for an array of precious artefacts that ranges from medieval paintings to modern glass.

# ST GEORGE'S BASILICA & CONVENT

*A bull's-blood-coloured baroque façade conceals a severe ancient interior, the Romanesque Basilica of St George (Bazilika a Klášter sv Jiří). The nuns have long since left their convent to the north, now a worthy setting for fine collections of Gothic, Renaissance and baroque painting and sculpture.*

**Bare basilica** The Basilica is the biggest church of its date in the Czech Lands, its twin towers and pale, sober stonework a reminder of the great antiquity of the Castle complex. Very well preserved after restoration, it is no longer a church but is now a concert venue, and the austere interior, a great hall with wooden ceiling, houses a small number of impressive artworks.

**Paintings and princesses** Founded in 973, St George's Convent was a prestigious institution, a place to which princesses and other young ladies of noble birth were sent to receive the best possible education. Shut down like many other religious houses in 1782 by Emperor Joseph (who turned it into a barracks), it had to await the coming of the Communists for its rehabilitation; they planned to turn it into a 'Museum of the Czechoslovak People'. A painfully long period of restoration has provided a more than adequate home for one of the country's greatest and most unique galleries, the National Gallery of Old Bohemian Art. In the Middle Ages, artists from Bohemia led Europe in their ability to convey the serene beauty of undisturbed faith; their sculpture and painting, displayed in the atmospheric setting of the convent's cellars, is unsurpassed. The upper floors contain the work of Prague's equally creative Renaissance and baroque periods.

## HIGHLIGHTS

- Sculpture of *St George and the Dragon*
- Krumlov's *Madonna and Child* sculpture
- Painted panels by the Master of Vyšší Brod
- Portraits of saints by Master Theodorik
- *Christ on the Mount of Olives* by the Třeboň Master
- Tympanum from Týn Church in Old Town
- Statue of Hercules
- *Tobias Restoring his Father's Sight* by Petr Brandl
- Landscapes by Roland Savary
- Genre scenes by Norbert Grund

## INFORMATION

- ✚ D4
- ✉ Jiřské náměsti, Hradčany
- ☎ 5732 0536
- ◷ Tue–Sun 10–6
- 🍴 Restaurants and cafés in Castle
- Ⓜ Malostranská, then an uphill walk
- 🚊 Tram 22 to Pražský hrad
- ♿ Few
- 🎫 Moderate
- ➡ Prague Castle (➤ 29)

31

**9**

# NERUDA STREET

*Toil up to the Castle from Malá Strana Square via steep, cobbled Neruda Street (Nerudova), and you will be rewarded by a sequence of exquisite town houses, baroque and rococo, on medieval foundations. Most have elaborate house signs.*

**Eagles and other emblems** It is the elegant façades and their emblems that catch the eye. There's an Eagle, Three Little Fiddles, a Goblet, a Golden Key and a Horseshoe. The Two Suns indicate the house (No 47) of author Jan Neruda (1843–91), who gave his name to the street; he was the Dickens of Malá Strana, a shrewd observer of the everyday life of the area. Most of the people who lived here were prosperous burghers, but there were some grandees, like the Morzins who built their palace at No 5 (the muscular Moors holding up the balcony are a pun on the family name). Their home is now an embassy, as is the Thun-Hohensteins' palace at No 20; here the Moors' job is being carried out by a pair of odd-looking eagles.

**Spur Street** The secret of savouring Neruda Street to the full is to coast gently downwards, like the coachmen from whom the road derived its earlier German name of Spornergasse (Spur Street), the spur in this case being the skid-like brake that slowed their otherwise precipitous progress down the steep slope.

## HIGHLIGHTS

- No 2, U kocoura (The Tomcat) pub
- No 5, Morzin Palace
- No 6, The Red Eagle
- No 12, The Three Little Fiddles
- No 16, The Golden Goblet
- No 20, Thun-Hohenstein Palace
- No 27, The Golden Key
- No 34, The Golden Horseshoe
- Baroque Church of Our Lady of Divine Providence
- No 47, The Two Suns, home of Jan Neruda

## INFORMATION

- ✚ C–D4
- ✉ Nerudova, Malá Strana
- 🍴 Restaurants and cafés
- 🚊 Tram 22 to Malá Strana Square (Malostranské náměstí)
- ♿ Few
- ↔ Prague Castle (➤ 29), St Nicholas's Church, Malá Strana (➤ 33)

*The Three Little Fiddles, No 12 Nerudova*

**10**

# St Nicholas's Church, Malá Strana

*As you crawl insect-like around the base of this cliff of a church you feel the full power of the Catholic Counter-Reformation expressing itself in what is surely one of the boldest and most beautiful baroque buildings of Central Europe.*

**Counter-Reformation citadel** When the Jesuits came to Prague following the rout of the Protestants at the Battle of the White Mountain, the existing little 13th-century church at the centre of Malá Strana Square was far too modest for their aspirations. The new St Nicholas's Church (Chrám svatého Mikuláše) was eventually completed in the 18th century and, with its lofty walls and high dome and bell-tower, became one of the dominant features of the city. The Jesuits intended their church to impress, but not through size alone. They employed the finest architects of the day (the Dientzenhofers, father, and son, plus Anselmo Lurago), along with the most talented interior designers. The subtly undulating west front is adorned with statues proclaiming the triumph of the Jesuit Order under the patronage of the imperial House of Habsburg. Inside, no effort was spared to enthrall the eye – with the dynamic play of space, statuary and painting – and the ear – with words (declaimed from the fantastically decorated pulpit) and music (through the 2,500 pipes of the great organ).

**Princely palaces and humbler households** In front of the church swirls the life of Malá Strana, locals waiting for the trams mixing with tourists following the Royal Way (▶ 16). Malá Strana Square is lined with a fascinating mixture of ancient town houses and grand palaces, while attached to St Nicholas's is the Jesuits' college, now part of the University.

## HIGHLIGHTS

**St Nicholas's Church**
- West front
- St Barbara's Chapel
- Organ with fresco of St Cecilia
- Dome with Holy Trinity fresco
- Huge sculptures of four Church Fathers
- *Trompe-l'oeil* ceiling fresco by Kracker

**Malá Strana Square**
- Arcaded houses
- No 10, Renaissance house
- No 13, Liechtenstein Palace of 1791
- Nos 18 and 19, Smiřický Palace and Šternberg House

## INFORMATION

- D4
- Malostranské náměstí
- Apr–Sep daily 9–5. Oct–Mar daily 9–4:30
- Restaurants and cafés in square
- Malostranská
- Tram 12, 22 to Malostranské náměstí
- Few
- Cheap
- Neruda Street (▶ 32), Wallenstein Palace (▶ 34), Charles Bridge (▶ 35)

**11**

# WALLENSTEIN PALACE

## HIGHLIGHTS

- Sala Terrena
- Garden sculptures (copies of originals by de Vries)
- Grotesquery and aviary in garden
- Riding School (museum with temporary exhibitions)

## INFORMATION

- D4
- Valdštejnské náměstí, Malá Strana
- Palace: closed to the public. Garden: May–Oct
- Malostranská
- Few
- Free
- Neruda Street (➤ 32), St Nicholas's Church, Malá Strana (➤ 33)

*Think of this palace – Prague's biggest – as an awful warning, an admonition to eschew excessive ambition and arrogance of the kind shown by its builder, Albrecht von Wallenstein, whose aspirations to power and fame led to his assassination.*

**Greedy generalissimo** Wallenstein's huge late Renaissance/early baroque palace (Valdštejnský palác) crouches at the foot of Prague Castle as if waiting to gobble it up. A whole city block, previously occupied by a couple of dozen houses and a brickworks, was demolished to make way for the complex of five courtyards, a barracks, a riding school and a superb garden that were intended to reflect Wallenstein's wealth and status. Wallenstein (Valdštejn in Czech) turned the troubled times of the early 17th century to his advantage. Having wormed his way into the emperor's favour, he became Governor of Prague, then Duke of Friedland. He married for money (twice), and great tracts of land (even whole towns) fell into his hands following the Battle of the White Mountain in 1620. His fortunes grew further as he quartermastered the imperial armies as well as leading them. Rightly suspicious of his subject's intentions – Wallenstein was negotiating with the enemy – the emperor had him killed.

**The general's garden** The Great Hall of the palace, with its ceiling painting of Wallenstein as Mars, the god of war, can only be seen if you have friends in the Czech Senate, which now occupies the building. The formal garden is more freely accessible. The latter is dominated by the superb Sala Terrena loggia, modelled on those in Italy, and has convincing copies of the statues stolen by Swedish soldiers during the Thirty Years War.

**12**

# CHARLES BRIDGE

*Any time is right for a visit to Prague's magnificent medieval bridge over the River Vltava. Enjoy the antics of the hucksters, then return at dusk to see the sculpted saints along the parapets gesticulating against the darkening sky.*

**Gothic flyover** For centuries the Charles Bridge (Karlův most) was Prague's only bridge, built on the orders of Emperor Charles IV in the 14th century. It's a triumph of Gothic engineering, 16 massive sandstone arches carrying it more than 500m from the Old Town across the Vltava River to touch down almost in the heart of Malá Strana. The bridge is protected by sturdy timber cutwaters and guarded at both ends by towers. The eastern face of the Old Town Bridge Tower is richly ornamented; its opposite number is accompanied by a smaller tower, once part of the earlier Judith Bridge.

**Starry saint** Charles Bridge has always been much more than a river crossing. Today's traders succeed earlier merchants and stallholders, and tournaments, battles and executions have all been held on the bridge. The heads of the Protestants executed in 1621 in Old Town Square were displayed here. Later that century the bridge was beautified with baroque sculptures, including the statue of St John Nepomuk. Falling foul of the king, this unfortunate cleric was pushed off the bridge in a sack. As his body bobbed in the water, five stars danced on the surface. Nepomuk hence became the patron saint of bridges, and is always depicted with his starry halo.

## HIGHLIGHTS

- Old Town Bridge Tower
- Malá Strana Bridge Tower (viewpoint)
- Nepomuk statue with bronze relief panels
- Bruncvík (Roland column) to south-west
- Statue of St John of Matha
- Bronze crucifix with Hebrew inscription
- Statue of St Luitgard (by Braun)

## INFORMATION

- ✚ D4
- Ⓜ Staroměstská
- 🚋 Tram 12, 22 to Malá Strana Square
- ♿ Good
- ↔ St Nicholas's Church, Malá Strana (► 33)

*St Anthony of Padua*

**13**

# NATIONAL THEATRE

## INFORMATION

➕ D/E5
✉ Národní 2, Nové město
☎ 24 91 34 37
🍴 Bar
Ⓜ Národní třída
♿ Few
↔ Bethlehem Chapel (➤ 55)

*The National Theatre reflected in the River Vltava*

*Even if the thought of a classical play per-formed in Czech doesn't enthrall you, don't miss the National Theatre (Národní divadlo). It is, perhaps, the greatest of Prague's collective works of art, decorated by the finest artists of the age.*

**National drama** In the mid-19th century, theatre in Prague still spoke with a German voice. Money to build a specifically Czech theatre was collected from 1849 onwards, without sup-port from German-dominated officialdom. The foundation stone was laid in 1868 with much festivity, then in 1881, just before the first performance, the whole place burnt down. Undiscouraged, the populace rallied, and by 1893 the theatre had been completely rebuilt. The opening was celebrated with a grand gala performance of the opera *Libuše* by Smetana, a passionate supporter of the theatre project.

**Expanded ambition** The National Theatre stands at the New Town end of the Legions Bridge (most Legií), its bulk carefully angled to fit into the streetscape and not diminish the view to Petřín Hill on the far bank. It was given a long-deserved restoration in time for its centenary, and when it reopened in 1983 it had gained a piazza and three annexes, whose architecture has been

much maligned, the least unkind comment being that the build-ings seem to be clad in bubble-wrap. Prague's well-known Laterna Magika multimedia show performs in one of these additional buildings, the Nova scéna.

# DECORATIVE ARTS MUSEUM

*Don't be put off by the uninviting building or the forlornly flapping banner that proclaims the museum's name (Uměleckoprůmyslové muzeum). At the top of a steep flight of stairs are little-visited treasure chambers full of fine furniture, glass, porcelain, clocks, metal-work and more...*

**Riverside reclaimed** Looking something like a miniature Louvre, the museum was built in 1901 in an area that, by the end of the 19th century, had turned its back on the river and had become a jumble of storage depots and timber yards. The city fathers determined to beautify it with fine public buildings and riverside promenades on the Parisian model. The School of Arts and Crafts (1884) and the House of Artists (1890) preceded the Decorative Arts Museum; the University's Philosophy Building (1929), which completed the enclosure of what is now Jan Palach Square, followed it.

**Decorative delights** The museum's collections are incredibly rich and diverse, numbering nearly 200,000 items. Unfortunately, only a fraction has ever been on display at any one time. In particular, the extraordinary Czech contribution to the development of 20th-century art and design has never been dealt with adequately, a situation that has recently been remedied partly by the opening of the Museum of Modern Art (► 47). In the meantime, the Decorative Arts Museum offers antiques enthusiasts a treat. Although the museum's scope is international, the focus is on the beautiful objects originating in the Czech Lands from Renaissance times to the 19th century. They are displayed in an endearingly old-fashioned way, in sumptuous settings.

## HIGHLIGHTS

- Pietra dura scene of a town by Castnicci
- Beer glasses engraved with card players
- Boulle commode and cabinet
- Monumental baroque furniture by Dientzenhofer and Santini
- Meissen Turk on a rhino
- Holic porcelain figures
- Harrachov glass
- Klášterec figurines of Prague characters
- Biedermeier cradle
- Surprise view down into the Old Jewish Cemetery

## INFORMATION

- ➕ E4
- ✉ 17 listopadu 2, Staré město
- ☎ 24 81 12 41
- 🕐 Tue–Sun 10–6
- 🍴 Café: (🕐 Mon–Fri 10–6; Sat–Sun 10:30–6)
- Ⓜ Staroměstská
- ♿ Few
- 🎫 Moderate
- ↔ Old/New Synagogue, Josefov (► 39), Old Jewish Cemetery (► 40)

**15**

# VYŠEHRAD

*Rising high above the River Vltava is Vyšehrad ('High Castle'), where the soothsaying Princess Libuše foresaw the founding of Prague, 'a city whose splendour shall reach unto the stars', and where she married her ploughman swain, Přemysl.*

**Romantic rock** Beneath Vyšehrad's 19th-century neo-Gothic Church of St Peter and St Paul are the remains of a far earlier, Romanesque church that once served the royal court. But it was in the 19th century, with the rise of Romantic ideas about history and nationhood, that poets, painters and playwrights celebrated the great fortress-rock, elaborating the story of Libuše. Most of their efforts have been forgotten, though Smetana's 'Vyšehrad', part of his glorious tone-poem *Má vlast*, is still popular. The nation's great and

*Devil's Pillars, Karlach's Park*

good have been buried in the Slavín, the National Cemetery (or Pantheon) at Vyšehrad, since the late 19th century. Smetana himself is here, along with fellow-composer Dvořák.

**Vltava views** Everyone driving along the main riverside highway has to pay homage to Vyšehrad, as the road and tram tracks twist and turn and then tunnel through the high rock protruding into the Vltava. In the 1920s the whole hilltop was turned into a public park, with wonderful views up and down the river (▶ 51).

**16**

# OLD/NEW SYNAGOGUE, JOSEFOV

*To step down from the street through the low portal of Josefov's Old/New Synagogue (Staronová synagóga) is to enter another world, one which endured a thousand years until brought to a tragic end by Nazi occupation.*

**Ghetto memories** The Old/New Synagogue stands at the heart of Josefov, the former Jewish Ghetto. Prague's Jews moved here in the 13th century; by that time they had already lived at various locations in the city for hundreds of years. High walls kept the Jews in and their Christian neighbours out, though not in 1389, when 3,000 Jews died in a vicious pogrom and the Synagogue's floor ran with blood. The ghetto community produced some extraordinary characters, such as Rabbi Loew, Renaissance scholar, confidant of emperors and creator of that archetypal man-made monster, the Golem. Moulded from river mud, the mournful Golem first served his master dutifully, but eventually ran amok until the rabbi managed to calm him down. Legend has it that the monster's remains are hidden in the Synagogue's loft. Far worse monsters marched in as the Germans annexed Czechoslovakia in 1939; by the end of World War II most of the country's Jews had perished, some in the Czech prison town of Terezín/Theresienstadt, the majority in Auschwitz.

**Ghetto Gothic** With its pointed brick gable and atmospheric interior, the Gothic Old/New Synagogue of 1275 is the oldest building of its kind north of the Alps, a compelling reminder of the age-old intertwining of Jewish and Christian culture in Europe. Remember that for Prague's few remaining Jews it is not a museum but still a place of worship.

## HIGHLIGHTS

- Vine carving in entrance portal
- Unconventional five-ribbed vaults
- Gothic grille of the *bimah* (pulpit)
- Rabbi Loew's seat
- Imperial banner recognising Jewish bravery in the Thirty Years War
- Ark with foliage carving

## INFORMATION

- E4
- Pařížská and Červená
- Jan–Mar, Nov–Dec Sun–Thu 9–4:30; Fri 9–2. Apr–Oct Sun–Thu 9–6; Fri 9–5
- Restaurant in Jewish Town Hall
- Staroměstská
- Few
- Moderate
- Decorative Arts Museum (▶ 37), Old Jewish Cemetery (▶ 40), Old Town Square (▶ 42)

# OLD JEWISH CEMETERY

*Just as the sunlight filtering through the tall trees is reduced to a dappled shade, so visitors' voices diminish to a hush as they contemplate the 12,000 toppling tombstones of this ancient burial place (Starý židovský hřbitov).*

## HIGHLIGHTS

**Around the cemetery**
- Jewish Town Hall with Hebraic clock
- Klausen Synagogue (Jewish traditions exhibit)
- Ceremonial Hall
- Pinkas Synagogue (77,297 names of Holocaust victims; pictures from Ferezin/Theresienstadt)
- Statue of Rabbi Loew on New Town Hall, Old Town

**In the cemetery**
- Tombstone of Rabbi Loew (c1525–1609)
- Tombstone of Mayor Maisel (1528–1601)

## INFORMATION

- E4
- U starého hřbitova, Staré město
- State Jewish Museum: 231 7191
- Sun–Fri 9–4:30
- Restaurant in Jewish Town Hall
- Staroměstská
- None
- Moderate
- Decorative Arts Museum (➤ 37), Old/New Synagogue, Josefov (➤ 39), Old Town Square (➤ 42)

**The changing Ghetto** Over the centuries the Jewish Ghetto, hemmed in by its walls, became intolerably crowded. By the time Emperor Joseph II gave the Jews partial emancipation towards the end of the 18th century, the Ghetto had 12,000 inhabitants, crammed together within it in increasingly sordid conditions. During the course of the 19th century many moved out to more salubrious quarters in the suburbs. Around 1900, the city fathers decided to 'improve' the Ghetto, by then named Josefov ('Joseph's Town') in honour of the emperor. Most of it was flattened to make way for broad streets and boulevards, though the rococo Jewish Town Hall and a clutch of synagogues around the cemetery were spared. They survived under the German occupation, because Hitler hoped to preserve what was left of the Ghetto as a 'Museum of a Vanished Race'. The stolen valuables of the Jewish communities of Bohemia and Moravia were brought to Prague, where some are now on display in the synagogues administered by the State Jewish Museum.

**Solemn cemetery** The cemetery is evocative of the long centuries of Jewish life in Prague. Unable to extend it, the custodians were forced to bury the dead one on top of the other, up to 12 deep in places. The total number laid to rest here may amount to 80,000. Visitors leave wishful notes under pebbles on the more prominent tombstones (like that of Rabbi Loew).

# ST AGNES'S CONVENT

*A few years ago it seemed unlikely that the restoration of St Agnes's Convent (Anežský klášter) would ever be finished. However, the city's most venerable Gothic complex is now open to the public at last, a fit setting for a fascinating and unfamiliar art collection.*

**Canonised Czech** Agnes was a 13th-century princess, sister of Wenceslas I and founder of a convent of Poor Clares here. In its glory days the convent was a mausoleum for the royal family, but was sacked by the Hussites in the 15th century. In 1782 it was closed down by Joseph II, and for more than a century it became a slum, its noble interior partitioned and crammed with tenants. At the turn of the century, the convent was saved from demolition by public protest. It was another hundred years before it was restored – by the Communists. On 12 November 1989, just days before their demise, Agnes was made a saint. An auspicious augury?

**Czech collection** The convent now houses the National Gallery's extensive collections of 19th-century Czech art. Look out for works by Josef Mánes (painter and revolutionary), Mikóláš Aleš (painter and graphic artist), Josef Myslbek (sculptor and graphic artist) and Jakub Schikaneder, a painter of atmospheric urban scenes.

## HIGHLIGHTS

- Rustic idyll *Below the Cottage*, Josef Mánes
- History painting *Oldřich and Božena*, F Ženíšek
- *Winter Evening in Town*, Jakub Schikaneder
- Study for the Wenceslas statue, Josef Václav Myslbek
- *Primeval Forest*, Julius Mařák
- Vaulted medieval cloister
- Church of St Francis (concert hall)
- Church of the Holy Saviour

## INFORMATION

- ✛ E3
- ✉ U milosrdných 17, Staré město
- ☎ 24 81 06 28
- 🕐 Tue–Sun 10–6
- 🍴 Café
- Ⓜ Staroměstská
- 🚋 Tram 17 (Právnická fakulta stop) or Tram 5, 14 (Dlouhá třída stop)
- ♿ Few
- 💷 Moderate
- ↔ Postal Museum (► 53)

Below the Cottage, *by Josef Mánes*

# OLD TOWN SQUARE

## HIGHLIGHTS

- Astronomical Clock (Orloj) from the 15th century (➤ 59)
- Council Hall and Clock Tower (➤ 50) of Old Town Hall
- Sgraffitoed House at the Minute, dated 1611 (No 2)
- Baroque Church of St Nicholas
- Jan Hus Memorial of 1915
- Pavement crosses in front of Old Town Hall
- Goltz-Kinský Palace (Graphic Art Collection; ➤ 52)
- Gothic House at the Stone Bell (➤ 52)
- Renaissance house (No 14)
- Arcaded houses (Nos 22–6), with baroque façades and medieval interiors and cellars

## INFORMATION

- E4
- Staroměstské náměstí, Staré město
- Cafés and restaurants
- Staroměstská
- Fair
- Old/New Synagogue, Josefov (➤ 39)

*Visitors throng this spacious square (Staroměstské náměstí) at all times of year, entertained by buskers, refreshed at outdoor cafés and enchanted by the Astronomical Clock and the cheerful façades of the old buildings.*

*Square and Týn Church*

**Martyrs and mournful memories** The Old Town Square has not always been so jolly. The medieval marketplace became a scene of execution, where Hussites lost their heads in the 15th century and 27 prominent Protestants were put to death in 1621 (they are commemorated by white crosses in the paving). In 1945, in a final act of spite, diehard Nazis demolished a whole wing of the Old Town Hall; the site has still not been built on. On 21 February 1948, Premier Gottwald proclaimed the triumph of Communism from the rococo Goltz-Kinský Palace.

**Round the square** The hub of the square is the Jan Hus Memorial, an extraordinary art nouveau sculpture whose base is one of the few places in the square where you can sit without having to buy a drink! From here, to your left rise the blackened towers of the Týn Church, while to your right is the Old Town Hall, an attractively varied assembly of buildings and, further round, the city's second St Nicholas's Church. The fine town houses surrounding the square are a study in different architectural styles, ranging from the genuine Gothic of the House at the Stone Bell to the 19th-century mock-Gothic of No 16.

# WENCESLAS SQUARE

*Despite its sometimes rather seedy air, Wenceslas Square (Václavské náměstí) is still the place where the city's heart beats most strongly, and to meet someone 'beneath the horse' (the Wenceslas statue) remains a special thrill.*

**When is a square not a square?** When it's a boulevard. 'Václavák', 700m long, slopes gently up to the imposing façade of the National Museum (▶ 44), which is fronted by the statue of Wenceslas on his sprightly steed. This is a good place to arrange a rendezvous – whatever the time of day there's always some action, with daytime shoppers and sightseers replaced by every species of night-owl as darkness falls.

Many of the dramas of modern times have been played out here. In 1918 the new state of Czechoslovakia was proclaimed, and in 1939 German tanks underlined the Republic's demise. In 1968, more tanks arrived – this time to crush the Prague Spring of Alexander Dubček. In protest at the Soviet occupation, Jan Palach burnt himself to death here the following year, and in 1989 Dubček and Václav Havel waved from the balcony of No 36 as half a million Czechs crowded the square to celebrate the collapse of Communism.

**Museum of modern architecture** The procession of buildings lining both sides of the square, from the resplendent art-nouveau Hotel Evropa to the elegant Functionalist Bata Store, tells the story of the distinctively Czech contribution to 20th-century architecture and design. Even more intriguing are the arcades (*pasáž*) that burrow deep into the buildings, creating a labyrinthine world of boutiques, theatres, cafés and cinemas.

## HIGHLIGHTS

- *St Wenceslas* statue, Josef Václav Myslbek (1912)
- Arcades of the Lucerna Palace
- Grand Hotel Evropa, completed 1905 (No 25)
- 1920s Functionalist Bata and Lindt buildings (No 25)
- Ambassador, late art-nouveau hotel of 1912 (No 5)
- Memorial to the victims of Communism
- 1950s Soviet-style Jalta Hotel (No 45)
- Former Bank of Moravia of 1916 (Nos 38–40)
- Art-nouveau Peterka building of 1901 (No 12)
- Koruna Palace of 1914 (No 1)

## INFORMATION

- E4–F5
- Václavské náměstí, Nové město
- Many cafés and restaurants
- Můstek or Muzeum
- Fair

21

# NATIONAL MUSEUM

*Some people find Prague's National Museum (Národní muzeum) disappointing, crammed as it is with cabinets full of beetles and mineral specimens. However, try to enjoy it as a period piece in its own right, for its dusty showcases are as venerable as the building itself.*

**Top building** With a gilded dome crowning the rise at the top of Wenceslas Square, the National Museum provides a grand finale to the capital's most important street. The neo-Renaissance building was completed in 1891, and at the time was as much an object of pride to the Czech populace as the National Theatre (➤ 36). Such is its presence that some visitors have mistaken it for the Parliament building, as did the Soviet gunner who raked its façade with machine-gun fire in August 1968.

**An array of -ologies** Even if you are not an enthusiastic entomologist, palaeontologist, zoologist, mineralogist or numismatist, you can't fail to be impressed by the evidence assembled here of the 19th century's great passion for collecting and classifying. Perhaps more immediately attractive for the casual visitor will be the temporary exhibitions, which draw on the museum's vast collections. The dinosaur display proves at least as compelling to young visitors as the famous film that may have

*Allegorical figure of the River Vltava, on the stairway leading up to the National Museum*

inspired it. Above all, the building itself is a most impressive exhibit, with its grand stairways, statuary, mosaics and patterned floors. And, unlike virtually every other attraction in Prague, it's open on Mondays!

**22**

# NATIONAL TECHNICAL MUSEUM

*Did you know that Czechoslovakia had one of the world's biggest auto industries and that Škoda cars were a byword for toughness and reliability? That a horse-drawn railway once linked Bohemia with Austria? That a Czechoslovak fleet once sailed the oceans?*

**Past glories** The answer to all these questions could be 'yes', based on evidence piled high in this wonderful museum (Národní technické muzeum), located off the beaten track on the edge of Letná Plain. The facelessness of the building belies the richness and fascination of its contents, a celebration of the longstanding technological prowess of inventive and hard-working Czechs. The Czech Lands were the industrial powerhouse of the Austro-Hungarian Empire, steel works and coal mines providing the foundation for excellence in engineering of all kinds, from the production of weapons to locomotive manufacture. Later, between the two world wars, independent Czechoslovakia's light industries led the world in innovativeness and quality.

**Trains and boats and planes** The museum's collection of technological artefacts is displayed to spectacular effect in the vast glass-roofed and galleried main hall, where balloons and biplanes hang in space above ranks of sinister-looking streamlined limousines and powerful steam engines. The side galleries tell the story of 'The Wheel' and of navigation, from rafting timber on the Vltava to transporting ore across the oceans in the Czechoslovak carrier *Košice*. Deep underground there's a mock-up of a coal mine, and other sections tell you all you ever wanted to know about time, sound, geodesy, photography and astronomy.

## HIGHLIGHTS

- 1928 Škoda fire engine
- Laurent and Klement soft-top roadster
- President Masaryk's V-12 Tatra
- Soviet ZIS 110B limousine
- Express locomotive 375-007 of 1911
- Imperial family's railway dining-car of 1891
- Bleriot XI Kašpar monoplane
- Sokol monoplane

## INFORMATION

- E3
- Kostelní 42/44, Holešovice
- 2039 9111
- Tue–Sun 9–5
- Tram 26 to Letenské náměstí, or Metro Vltavská then Tram 1 to Letenské náměstí
- Few
- Moderate
- Museum of Modern Art (➤ 47), Letná Plain (➤ 50)

# MUNICIPAL HOUSE

*The prosaic name 'Municipal House' fails utterly to convey anything of the character of the extraordinary art-nouveau Obecní dům, a gloriously extravagant turn-of-the-century confection on which every artist of the day seems to have left his stamp.*

**City council citadel** Glittering like some gigantic, flamboyant jewel, more brightly than ever since its restoration in 1997, the Obecní dům is linked to the blackened Powder Tower (Prašná brána; ➤ 51), last relic of the Old Town's fortifications and for long one of the city's main symbols. The intention of the city fathers in the first years of the 20th century was to add an even more powerful element to the cityscape which would celebrate the glory of the Czech nation and Prague's place within it. The site of the old Royal Palace was selected, and no expense was spared to erect a megastructure in which the city's burgeoning life could expand.

**Ornamental orgy** The building programme included meeting and assembly rooms, cafés, restaurants, bars, even a pâtisserie, while the mayor was provided with particularly luxurious quarters. The 1,149-seat Smetana Hall, later the home of the Czech Philharmonic, is a temple to the muse of Bohemian music. Everything, even the lifts, is encrusted with the most lavish decoration in stucco, metal-work, glass, mosaic, murals and textiles.

*The glittering portal of the Municipal House*

**24**

# MUSEUM OF MODERN ART

*'What I found to be a truly great experience was a tour of the Prague Trades Fair Building. The first impression created by the enormous palace is breathtaking.' So enthused the great architect Le Corbusier, when he visited Prague in 1928 shortly after this monumental structure, the Veletržní Palác, was completed.*

**Trail-blazer** Never lacking in ego, Le Corbusier was none the less vexed to find that his Czech colleagues had pipped him to the post in completing what is one of the key buildings in the evolution of 20th-century design, a secular, modern-day cathedral constructed in concrete, steel and glass. Set in the suburb of Holešovice, the palace was intended to be a showpiece for the products of Czechoslovakia. However, trade fairs moved away from Prague to Brno, and for many years the great building languished in neglect and obscurity, its originality forgotten as its architectural innovations became the norm throughout the world.

**Disguised blessing** After fire gutted the palace in 1974, it was decided to use its elegant spaces to display the city's modern art treasures, which had previously been hidden away without a proper home. In all, it took nearly 20 years to complete restoration work, but the wait was well worth while. The core of the collection remains the amazing achievements of Czech painters and sculptors in the early part of the 20th century. It also shows works by the French Impressionists and other modern foreign paintings from the National Gallery, and promotes contemporary arts of all types, staging the kind of major international art shows of which the Czechs were so long deprived.

## HIGHLIGHTS

- *Reader of Dostoyevsky,* Emil Filla
- *Serie C VI,* František Kupka
- *Melancholy,* Jan Zrzavý
- *Sailor,* Karel Dvořák
- *Self-portrait,* Picasso
- *Self-portrait,* Douanier Rousseau
- *Green Rye,* Van Gogh
- *Virgin,* Gustav Klimt
- *Pregnant Woman and Death,* Egon Schiele

## INFORMATION

- F2
- Dukelských hrdinů 47, Holešovice
- 24 30 11 11
- Tue–Wed, Fri–Sun 10–6; Thu 10–9
- Restaurants and cafés
- Tram 5 from Náměstí Republiky
- Few
- Moderate
- National Technical Museum (► 45)

*Top:* Green Rye *by Van Gogh*

**25**

# TROJA CHÂTEAU

*Out here you can catch a glimpse of how delightful Prague's countryside must have been three centuries ago, with vine-clad slopes, trees in abundance and the resplendent baroque palace of Trojský zámek set among allées and parterres.*

**Prague's Versailles** This extravagant palace was built not by the monarch, but by the second richest man in Prague, Count Wenceslas Adelbert Šternberg. The Šternbergs profited from the Thirty Years War, and at the end of the 17th century were in a position to commission Jean-Baptiste Mathey to design a country house along the lines of the contemporary châteaux of the architect's native France. The south-facing site by the river, orientated directly on St Vitus's Cathedral and Prague Castle on the far side of the Royal Hunting Grounds (now Stromovka Park), was ideal for Šternberg, allowing him to offer the monarch the right kind of hospitality following a day's hunting.

**Ornamental extravagance** The palace's proportions are grandiose, and its painted interiors go over the top in paying homage to the country's Habsburg rulers. And over the top, too, goes a turbaned Turk as he topples, in stunning *trompe-l'oeil*, from the mock battlements in the Grand Hall. Troja was acquired by the state in the 1920s, but restored only in the late 1980s (some think excessively). It contains part of Prague's collection of 19th-century paintings, few of which can compete with the flamboyance of their setting.

*Ornamentation at Troja*

# PRAGUE's
## *best*

# PANORAMAS

## Across the river

Some of the finest views of Prague are those in which the city is seen across the broad waters of the Vltava, as from the Smetana statue or Kampa Island. A stroll along the embankments and footpaths on both sides of the river is equally rewarding, as are the islands – Slavonic Island (Slovanský ostrov) and Shooters' Island (Střelecký ostrov).

*Malá Strana from Petřín*

### TOWER, ST VITUS'S CATHEDRAL (KATEDRÁLA SVATÉHO VÍTA)
Climb the tower's 287 steps for one of the best all-round panoramas of the city and its surroundings, as well as close-ups of the intricate exterior of the Cathedral itself, with its bristling buttresses, diamond-tiled roofs and copper cockerels atop spiky perches.
🕀 C/D4 ⊠ Pražský hrad ⏰ Apr–Oct daily 10–5 🍴 Cafés and restaurants 🚊 Tram 22 to Pražský hrad 👎 Cheap

### EMBANKMENT, KAMPA ISLAND
From the shady parkland of Kampa Island there is an unusual view across the Vltava over Charles Bridge and the foaming weir to the Old Town.
🕀 D4 ⊠ U Sovových mlýnů ⏰ Permanently open 🚊 Trams 12, 22 to Hellichova 👎 Free

### LETNÁ PLAIN (LETENSKÉ SADY)
The parks and gardens of Letná Plain stretch from the eastern end of Prague Castle high above the north bank of the Vltava. Between 1955 and 1962 a monster statue of Stalin stood here. The plinth, now infested with skateboarders, is occupied by a giant metronome, and makes an excellent vantage point over the river, its bridges and the Old Town.
🕀 D–E3 ⊠ Letenské sady ⏰ Permanently accessible
Ⓜ Malostranská then uphill walk 🚊 Tram 18 to Chotkovy sady or 22 to Kralovský letohrádek 👎 Free

### OLD ROYAL PALACE (STARÝ KRÁLOVSKÝ PALÁC)
After admiring the interiors of the Old Royal Palace and the Vladislav Hall, take a stroll on the south-facing terrace or peep out of the windows from which the Catholic councillors were thrown out in 1618 (► 12). All Prague lies at your feet.
🕀 D4 ⊠ Pražský hrad ☎ 2437 3368 ⏰ Apr–Oct Tue–Sun 9–5. Nov–Mar Tue–Sun 9–4 🍴 Cafés and restaurants 🚊 Tram 22 to Pražský hrad 👎 Moderate

### TOWER, OLD TOWN HALL (STAROMĚSTSKÁ RADNICE)
The climb up the tower of the Old Town Hall is well worth while for the dizzying view it gives of the swarming activity in Old Town Square below, as well as of the higgledy-piggledy red-tiled roofs of the medieval Old Town.
🕀 E4 ⊠ Staroměstské náměstí ☎ 2448 3254 ⏰ Apr–Sep Mon 11–6; Tue–Sun 9–6. Oct–Mar Mon 11–5; Tue–Sun 9–5 🍴 Restaurants in Square Ⓜ Staroměstská 👎 Moderate

### PETŘÍN HILL LOOKOUT TOWER (ROZHLEDNA)
This little brother of the Eiffel Tower was erected for Prague's great Jubilee Expo of 1891. Prepare to climb 299 steps!

⊞ C4  ☒ Petřín  🕙 Apr–Aug daily 10–7. Sep–Oct daily 10–6. Nov–Mar Sat–Sun 10–5  🚋 Tram 12 or 22 to Hellichova, then Lanovka funicular (from Újezd)  💷 Moderate

### POWDER TOWER (PRAŠNÁ BRÁNA)
The sumptuous roofscape of the adjoining Obecní dům (Municipal House; ➤ 46) makes an immediate impact, but this panorama is particularly appealing because of the vista along Celetná Street into the heart of the Old Town.

⊞ E/F4  ☒ Náměstí Republiky  🕙 Winter daily 10–5. Summer daily 10–6  🚇 Náměstí Republiky  🚋 Trams 5, 14 to Náměstí Republiky  💷 Moderate

### SMETANA STATUE
The walkway leading to the Smetana Museum (➤ 57) is in fact a pier (known as Novotného lávka), built out into the river. At the very tip of the pier are café tables and a statue of the composer; the view across the river, whose roaring weir drowns all intrusive noises, is the classic one of Charles Bridge, Malá Strana and Prague Castle above.

⊞ D4  ☒ Novotného lávka  🕙 Permanently open  🍴 Café and restaurant  🚇 Staroměstsky  🚋 Trams 17, 18 to Karlovy lázně  💷 Free

### TELEVISION TOWER (TELEVIZNÍ VYSÍLAČ)
This immensely tall (216m) television transmitter tower in the inner suburb of Žižkov may be a blot on Prague's townscape (see panel), but its gallery does give visitors stupendous views over the city and its surroundings. The best time to take the lift to the top is fairly early in the day before the sun has got too far round to the west.

⊞ G5  ☒ Mahlerovy sady  ☎ 6700 5784  🍴 Restaurant  🚇 Jiřího z Poděbrad  🚋 Trams 5, 9, 26 to Lipanská  💷 Moderate

### VYŠEHRAD
A walk around the ramparts of the old fortifications of Vyšehrad gives contrasting views along the Vltava flowing far below. Upstream, Prague is surprisingly countrified, with rugged limestone crags and rough woodland, while downstream the panorama reveals the city, especially Hradčany, from an entirely new angle. Near by, the terraces of the Communists' huge Palace of Culture offer a view across the deep Nusle ravine towards the New Town, guarded by the walls and cupolas of the Karlov Monastery.

⊞ E6–7  ☒ Vyšehrad  🕙 Permanently accessible  🍴 Café and restaurant  🚇 Vyšehrad  🚋 Trams 3, 7, 17 to Výtoň

*Old Town Square from the Old Town Hall tower*

## Unpopular neighbour

Building the unlovely TV tower in Žižkov necessitated destroying part of an old Jewish cemetery and was resisted (in so far as any resistance was possible in Communist days) by locals and other protesters. Some people are still uneasy, claiming that they pick up transmissions on virtually any metal object, or that their bodies are being slowly microwaved.

51

# GALLERIES

## Unseen art

Housing Prague's vast and varied art collections has always posed problems. Under Communism, many pictures and other art objects were kept more or less permanently in store, and the unique Czech contribution to 20th-century art has never been properly celebrated. The big issue is now a financial one. If there are particular works you want to see it's worth checking first whether they are actually on display.

### GOLTZ-KINSKÝ PALACE (PALÁC GOLTZ-KINSKÝCH)

Changing exhibitions, based on the National Gallery's vast collections of prints and drawings. It was from a balcony here that Klement Gottwald proclaimed the victory of the working classes in 1948.
✚ E4 ⊠ Staroměstské náměstí 12 ☎ 24 81 07 58 ⏰ Reopening in 1999 after reconstruction 🍴 Cafés and restaurants in Old Town Square 🚇 Staroměstská 💰 Moderate

### HOUSE AT THE STONE BELL (DŮM U KAMENNÉHO ZVONU)

For many years this fine town house, now displaying art by young Czech contemporaries, was thought to be a rococo palace. When the restorers began work on it, that rarity, a Gothic mansion, was discovered behind the 18th-century work. After much debate, the building was restored to its medieval state.
✚ E4 ⊠ Staroměstské náměstí 13 ☎ 2482 7526 ⏰ Tue–Sun 10–6 🍴 Cafés and restaurants in Old Town Square 🚇 Staroměstská 💰 Moderate

*House at the Stone Bell*

### LAPIDÁRIUM

Classical and modern sculpture, including some of the original statues from Charles Bridge brought here to protect them.
✚ F2 ⊠ Výstaviště, Holešovice ☎ 2422 6488 ⏰ Fri 12–6; Sat–Sun 10–12:30, 1–6 🍴 Cafés and restaurants in grounds 🚇 Nádraží Holešovice 🚃 Trams 5, 12, 17 to Výstaviště 💰 Cheap

### RIDING SCHOOL OF PRAGUE CASTLE (JÍZDÁRNA)

This big baroque building is used by the National Gallery for staging temporary exhibitions.
✚ C3 ⊠ U Prašného mostu 55, Hradčany ☎ 2437 3368 ⏰ Tue–Sun 10–6 🍴 Cafés and restaurants in Castle 🚃 Tram 22 to Pražský hrad 💰 Moderate

# MUSEUMS

See Top 25 Sights for
**DECORATIVE ARTS MUSEUM ➤ 37**
**NATIONAL MUSEUM ➤ 44**
**NATIONAL TECHNICAL MUSEUM ➤ 45**
**STATE JEWISH MUSEUM ➤ 40**

## CITY MUSEUM (MUZEUM HLAVNÍHO MĚSTA PRAHY)

This pompous late 19th-century building contains exhibits telling the story of Prague's evolution from the earliest times. The star is an extraordinary scale model of the city as it was in the 1820s and 1830s, meticulously put together by a person of infinite patience called Antonín Langweil. Most of the extensive collections are in storage, but selections (posters, postcards, etc) are shown in rotation.

🔳 F4 ☒ Na poříčí 52, north Nové město ☎ 2481 6772
🕐 Tue–Sun 10–6 🚇 Florenc 🎫 Cheap

## MILITARY MUSEUM, SCHWARZENBERG PALACE (VOJENSKÉ MUZEUM)

Behind the stunning sgraffito façades of this Renaissance palace is an array of militaria of all kinds – guns, uniforms, models, paintings, maps – proving what a bloody battleground Bohemia always was.

🔳 C4 ☒ Hradčanské náměstí 2, Hradčany ☎ 2020 2020
🕐 May–Oct Tue–Sun 10–6 🚇 Malostranská 🚊 Tram 22 to Pražský hrad 🎫 Cheap

## NÁPRSTEK MUSEUM (NÁPRSTKOVO MUZEUM)

Surprisingly few visitors climb the stairs to the intriguing ethnographical exhibits assembled here by a 19th-century collector in love with the indigenous cultures of the Americas and Pacific.

🔳 E4 ☒ Betlémské náměstí 1, Staré město ☎ 24 21 45 37
🕐 Tue–Sun 9–12, 12:45–5:30 🚇 Staroměstská or Národní třída
🎫 Cheap

## POLICE MUSEUM (MUZEUM POLICIE ČR)

This museum recovered quickly from the collapse of the old order in 1989, and gives an upbeat account of Czech policing, with plenty of gore and weaponry on show in, incongruously, what was once the Karlov Monastery.

🔳 E6 ☒ Ke Karlovu 1, Nové město ☎ 29 52 09 🕐 Tue–Sun 10–5 🚇 I P Pavlova or Vyšehrad 🎫 Cheap

## POSTAL MUSEUM (POŠTOVNÍ MUZEUM)

A delightful little museum of great appeal, and not just to philatelists. It's housed in an attractive building with some charming 19th-century frescos.

🔳 F3 ☒ Nové mlýny 2, north Nové město ☎ 23 12 060
🕐 Tue–Sun 9–5 🚇 Náměstí Republiky, then Tram 5, 14 to Dlouhá třída 🎫 Cheap

### The big guns

Czech and Slovak involvement in the big conflict that never happened, the face-off of the Cold War, is chillingly displayed in the huge collection of military hardware on show at the Aircraft Museum (Letecké muzeum) at Kbely airfield on the city's eastern outskirts. Some of the aircraft date back to World War I, but above all it's the MiGs that remain in the memory.

### More militaria

Almost unknown abroad, the tale of Czech and Slovak involvement in the conflicts of the 20th century is told in the Museum of the Resistance and History of the Army (Muzeum odboje a dějin armády), at the foot of the National Memorial in the inner suburb of Žižkov.

# PALACES

## High diplomacy

The Anglophile and athletic first president of Czechoslovakia, Tomáš Masaryk, is reputed to have maintained good relations with the British ambassador in the Thun Palace by climbing down a ladder set against Prague Castle's walls to drop in for tea.

*Coat of arms, Archbishop's Palace*

## Auto sculpture

In the summer of 1989, the streets around the West German Embassy were clogged with Wartburgs and Trabants abandoned by their East German owners. The memorial to these stirring days lurks in the shrubbery in the Embassy garden – a fibreglass Trabant on mighty, seven-league legs.

> **See Top 25 Sights for**
> **ROYAL PALACE ➤ 29**
> **ŠTERNBERG PALACE ➤ 27**
> **WALLENSTEIN PALACE ➤ 34**

### ARCHBISHOP'S PALACE (ARCIBISKUPSKÝ PALÁC)
The lusciously restored rococo façade hides a truly sumptuous residence, unfortunately accessible only on special occasions.
➕ C4 ✉ Hradčanské náměstí 16 🕔 Not normally open to the public 🚃 Tram 22 to Pražský hrad

### ČERNÍN PALACE (ČERNÍNSKÝ PALÁC)
It was from this huge baroque structure (completed 1720), now the Foreign Ministry, that Jan Masaryk fell to his death in 1948.
➕ C4 ✉ Loretánské náměstí, Hradčany 🕔 Not open to the public 🚃 Tram 22 to Pohořelec

### HOUSE OF THE LORDS OF KUNŠTÁT AND PODĚBRADY (DŮM PÁNŮ Z KUNŠTÁTU A PODĚBRAD)
Possibly the most ancient interior accessible to the public is this 13th-century mansion of King George of Poděbrady.
➕ E4 ✉ Řetězová 3, Staré město 🕔 Summer daily 10–6. Closed winter 🚇 Staroměstská 💶 Cheap

### LOBKOVIC PALACE (LOBKOVICKÝ PALÁC)
This superb baroque structure (not to be confused with the Lobkovic Palace within the Castle precinct), the residence of the German ambassador, saw strange scenes in summer 1989, when it became a temporary home to thousands of East Germans seeking refuge.
➕ C4 ✉ Vlašská 19 🕔 Not open to the public 🚃 Tram 12, 22 to Malostranské náměstí

### SCHÖNBORN-COLLOREDO PALACE (SCHÖNBORNSKÝ PALÁC)
The US Embassy occupies a baroque palace whose grandeur equals that of the nearby German Embassy.
➕ D4 ✉ Tržiště 15, Malá Strana 🕔 Not open to the public 🚃 Tram 12, 22 to Malostranské náměstí

### SCHWARZENBERG PALACE ➤ 53

### THUN PALACE (THUNOVSKÝ PALÁC)
The British Embassy since 1918. Presented by the emperor in 1630 to Walter Leslie, a Scotsman, who had helped to assassinate Wallenstein, the emperor's great rival.
➕ D4 ✉ Thunovská 25, Malá Strana 🕔 Not open to the public 🚇 Malostranská

# Churches

See Top 25 Sights for
**LORETTO SHRINE ➤ 26**
**ST GEORGE'S BASILICA ➤ 31**
**ST NICHOLAS'S CHURCH, MALÁ STRANA ➤ 33**
**ST VITUS'S CATHEDRAL ➤ 30**

### BETHLEHEM CHAPEL (BETLÉMSKÁ KAPLE)

You must see this barn-like structure, where Jan Hus preached, to really appreciate the deeply nonconformist traditions so thoroughly obscured by centuries of imposed Catholicism. The baroque architecture is extravagant.

🔲 E4 ⊠ Betlémské náměstí, Staré město ⏰ Apr–Oct daily 9–6. Nov–Mar daily 9–5 🍴 Restaurants and cafés near by 🚇 Národní třída 🎫 Cheap

### CHURCH OF OUR LADY VICTORIOUS (KOSTEL PANNY MARIE VÍTĚZNÉ)

After Czech Protestantism had been crushed in 1621, this church became a centre of the Counter-Reformation, thanks not least to miracles wrought by the Bambino di Praga waxwork (see panel).

🔲 D4 ⊠ Karmelitská 9, Malá Strana ⏰ Daily 7–9 🚋 Tram 12, 22 to Malostranské náměstí

### ST JAMES'S CHURCH (KOSTEL SVATÉHO JAKUBA)

Beneath the baroque froth is an ancient Gothic church. The acoustics of the long nave are particularly impressive, and concerts held here are well attended.

🔲 E4 ⊠ Malá Štupartská, Staré město ⏰ Daily 9:30–4 🚇 Náměstí Republiky

### ST NICHOLAS'S CHURCH, OLD TOWN (KOSTEL SVATÉHO MIKULÁŠE, STARÉ MĚSTO)

St Nicholas's twin towers and grand dome are the work of the great baroque architect, Kilian Ignaz Dientzenhofer. His church is now one of the more prominent features of Old Town Square, but Dientzenhofer designed it to fit into the narrow street that once ran here.

🔲 E4 ⊠ Staroměstské náměstí, Staré město ⏰ Tue, Thu, Fri 10–12; Wed 10–12, 2–4; Sun 9:30–10:30, 11:30–12 🚇 Staroměstská

### TÝN CHURCH (KOSTEL PANNY MARIE PŘED TÝNEM)

The Gothic Týn Church's twin towers, among the city's best-known landmarks, stick up spikily behind the houses east of Old Town Square. Inside are some fascinating tombs.

🔲 E4 ⊠ Týnská and Celetná, Staré město ⏰ May only be open for services due to reconstruction 🍴 Cafés and restaurants near by 🚇 Staroměstská or Náměstí Republiky

*Týn Church*

## Rough justice

A withered hand hangs from the altar in St James's Church, severed by a butcher when the thief to whom it belonged was apprehended by the Virgin Mary, who refused to let go.

## Bambino di Praga

The Bambino di Praga was given to the Church of Our Lady Victorious in 1628 as part of the compulsory re-Catholicisation of the wayward Czechs. The miracles performed by the diminutive effigy of the infant Jesus are even more numerous than its 60 sumptuous changes of outfit.

55

# TWENTIETH-CENTURY BUILDINGS

See Top 25 Sights for
**MUNICIPAL HOUSE (OBECNÍ DŮM) ➤ 46
VELETRŽNÍ PALÁC, MUSEUM OF
MODERN ART ➤ 47**

## Art nouveau

The glorious effusions of art nouveau, with its use of sinuous lines and motifs from the natural world, mark the townscape all over Prague. The city rivals Vienna in the number of edifices built in this style, known here as Secession.

*The famous Black Madonna*

## Czech innovations

Art nouveau/Secession was an international style, but later Czech architects created unique movements of their own, such as Rondo-Cubism and the more sober, functionalist style that followed.

### BANK OF THE LEGIONS (BANKA LEGIÍ)

Czechoslovak legionaries fought on many fronts in World War I, and the sculptures decorating the façade of this handsome Rondo-Cubist (see panel) building of 1923 commemorate their exploits.
➕ F4 ✉ Na poříčí 24, north Nové město 🕒 Accessible during banking hours to customers of Komerční Banka 🚇 Náměstí Republiky

### CUBIST STREETLAMP

This extraordinary little object, an echo of Czech Cubism, still seems to vibrate with the artistic excitements that suffused metropolitan life in early 20th-century Prague.
➕ E5 ✉ Jungmannovo náměstí, Nové město 🚇 Můstek

### HOUSE AT THE BLACK MADONNA (DŮM U ČERNÉ MATKY BOŽÍ)

This striking example of Czech Cubist architecture, designed by Josef Gočár (1912), stands challengingly at the corner of Celetná Street in the heart of the Old Town, yet somehow manages to harmonise with its venerable surroundings. Look for the Black Madonna in her gilded cage.
➕ E4 ✉ Ovocný trh 19, Staré město 🕒 Art gallery: Tue–Sun 10–6 🍴 Restaurant 🚇 Náměstí Republiky 💷 Cheap

### MAIN STATION (HLAVNÍ NÁDRAŽÍ)

Above the modern concourses rise the richly ornamented art-nouveau buildings of Prague's main station (1909), originally named after Emperor Franz Josef, then after President Wilson.
➕ F4 ✉ Wilsonova 8, Nové město 🕒 24 hours 🍴 Buffet 🚇 Hlavní nádraží 💷 Free

### NOS 7 & 9 NÁRODNÍ TŘÍDA

Fascinating variations on the theme of art nouveau can be traced in the façades of these adjoining office buildings. Both were designed by Osvald Polívka; No 9 was built for the publisher Topič and No 7 for an insurance company.
➕ E5 ✉ Národní třída 7 & 9, Nové město 🚇 Národní třída

### U NOVÁKŮ

This lavishly decorated art-nouveau structure, now a casino, was built as a department store in 1903. The colourful mosaic, by Jan Preisler, flowing over its façade, represents Trade and Industry.
➕ E5 ✉ Vodičkova 30, Nové město 🕒 Open to customers of Varieté Praga 🍴 Restaurant 🚇 Můstek

# FOR MUSIC LOVERS

**See Top 25 Sights for**
**NATIONAL THEATRE**
**(NÁRODNÍ DIVADLO) ➤ 36**
**ST NICHOLAS'S CHURCH, MALÁ STRANA ➤ 33**

### DVOŘÁK MUSEUM (VILA AMERIKA)
This exquisite little villa was built for Count Michna in 1720 as a summer retreat, when this part of the New Town was still countryside. It now serves as a fascinating repository for Dvořák memorabilia (➤ 76).
🞢 E6 ⊠ Ke Karlovu 20, Nové město ☎ 29 82 14 🕐 Tue–Sun 10–5 🚇 I P Pavlova 🎟 Cheap

### DVOŘÁK'S BIRTHPLACE
Dvořák was born the son of an innkeeper in the unassuming little village of Nelahozeves on the Elbe River. His birthplace, at the foot of the Lobkovic family's huge Renaissance castle, is now a museum.
🞢 Off map, about 30km north-west of Prague ⊠ Nelahozeves 12 🕐 Tue–Sun 9–12, 2–5 🚉 Nelahozeves 🎟 Cheap

### ESTATES THEATRE (STAVOVSKÉ DIVADLO) ➤ 75

### MOZART MUSEUM (BERTRAMKA)
Mozart's closest friends in Prague were the Dušeks, the Bertramka their rural retreat. This is the place where the great composer dashed off the last lines of *Don Giovanni* before conducting its première in the Estates Theatre (➤ 75).
🞢 C6 ⊠ Mozartova 169, Smíchov ☎ 54 38 93 🕐 Apr–Oct daily 9:30–6. Nov–Mar daily 9:30–5 🚇 Anděl, then Tram 4, 7, 9 to Bertramka (one stop) 🎟 Cheap

### SMETANA HALL (SMETANOVA SÍŇ)
The highly decorated Smetana Hall is the grandest space in the Municipal House (➤ 46), with seating for 1,149. The Prague Spring music festival is heralded here every year with a rousing rendition of the symphonic poem *Má vlast* ('*My Country*').
🞢 E/F4 ⊠ Obecní dům, Náměstí Republiky ☎ 2200 2100 🕐 Check locally for times of guided tours 🍴 Café and restaurant 🚇 Náměstí Republiky

### SMETANA MUSEUM (MUSEUM BEDŘICHA SMETANY)
The museum dedicated to the composer of 'Vltava' is appropriately sited in a building which rises directly out of the river.
🞢 D4 ⊠ Novotného lávka 1, Staré město ☎ 2422 9075 🕐 Wed–Mon 10–5 🚇 Staroměstská

### STATE OPERA (STÁTNÍ OPERA PRAHA – SMETANA DIVADLO) ➤ 75

## A musical nation
Co Čech – to muzikant! ('All Czechs are musicians!') goes the saying, and this is certainly one of the most musical of nations. Eighteenth-century Bohemia supplied musicians and composers to the whole of Europe.

## Music for free
By all means go to concerts at the places listed on this page. But bear in mind that 'all Czechs are musicians', and enjoy the often very high-quality music made by street performers. If you keep your ears cocked, you may even catch one of tomorrow's virtuosi practising at an open window.

*Dvořák's piano, Vila Amerika*

57

# GREEN SPACES

See Top 25 Sights for
**PETŘÍN HILL ➤ 28**
**WALLENSTEIN GARDENS ➤ 34**

## Monkish retreat

The old garden of the Franciscan monks between Wenceslas Square (Václavské náměstí) and Jungmann Square (Jungmannovo náměstí), modernised by Prague Parks Department, makes a welcome oasis in the heart of the city.

### BAROQUE GARDENS BELOW THE CASTLE

The aristocrats in their palaces in Malá Strana at the foot of Prague Castle turned their interconnecting gardens into a paradise of arbours, gazebos, fountains and stairways. Now partially reopened after restoration, they can also be enjoyed from the Castle's Ramparts Garden above.

➕ D4 ✉ Pražský hrad, Hradčany 🕐 Daily 🚇 Malostranská 👋 Cheap

### KAMPA ISLAND

Kampa Island was flooded regularly until the Vltava was tamed in the 1950s, discouraging building and leaving large parts of it undeveloped.

➕ D4–5 🕐 At all times 🚊 Tram 12, 22 to Hellichova or Malostranské náměstí 👋 Free

### LETNÁ PLAIN (LETENSKÉ SADY) ➤ 50

### RAMPARTS GARDEN (ZAHRADA NA VALECH)

The gardens just to the south of Prague Castle were redesigned in the 1920s and embellished with sculptural objects, including a miniature pyramid.

➕ C–D4 ✉ Pražský hrad, Hradčany 🕐 Summer 10–6. Closed winter 🚇 Malostranská then uphill walk 🚊 Tram 22 to Pražský hrad 👋 Free

### ROYAL GARDENS (KRÁLOVSKÁ ZAHRADA)

Fine old trees and formal gardens make a superb setting for several pleasure pavilions to the north of the Castle: the baroque Riding School (➤ 52), the sgraffitoed Ball-Game Hall and the beautiful little Belvedere.

➕ C/D3 ✉ Královský letohrádek, Hradčany 🕐 Summer 10–6. Closed winter 🚊 Tram 22 to Královský letohrádek 👋 Free

*Stromovka Park, Holešovice*

## Charles Square

Charles Square (Karlovo náměstí) is more of a park than a square, and is a useful resting-place when pounding the pavements becomes too tiring in this spread-out part of town.

### VOJAN GARDENS (VOJANOVY SADY)

A quiet retreat hidden away behind Malá Strana.

➕ D4 ✉ U lužického semináře 🕐 Daily 8–7 🚇 Malostranská 👋 Free

### VRTBA GARDEN (VRTBOVSKÁ ZAHRADA)

This is Prague's finest individual baroque garden, with a splendid staircase, superb sculptures and a view over Malá Strana.

➕ D4 ✉ Karmelitská 18, Malá Strana 🕐 May–Jun, Sep–Oct daily 10–4. Jul–Aug daily 10–6 🚊 Tram 12, 22 to Malostranské náměstí

# ATTRACTIONS FOR CHILDREN

See Top 25 Sights for
**NATIONAL TECHNICAL MUSEUM ➤ 45**
**PETŘÍN HILL, WITH FUNICULAR,**
    **VIEWING TOWER, HALL OF MIRRORS,**
    **OBSERVATORY ➤ 28**

### ASTRONOMICAL CLOCK (ORLOJ)

Crowds gather every hour on the hour in front of the Old Town Hall to enjoy the performance put on by this fascinating clock, which not only tells the time but gives the position of the sun, moon and much more, while the splendid painted calendar shows saints' days, the signs of the zodiac and the labours of the months. Legend has it that Hanuš, the master technician who perfected the mechanism, was blinded by the city fathers to stop him passing his secrets on. But Hanuš persuaded an apprentice to lead him up inside the clock. He then plunged his hands into the mechanism, putting it out of action for 80 years.

🔲 E4 ⊠ Staroměstské náměstí ⏰ Performances daily on the hour 9–9 🚇 Staroměstská 💰 Free

### CHANGING OF THE GUARD

The blue-uniformed Castle Guard is ceremonially relieved every day at noon, with extra helpings of buglers and pomp on Sundays.

🔲 C4 ⊠ Pražský hrad, Hradčany ⏰ Daily at noon 🚋 Tram 22 to Pražský hrad 💰 Free

### EXHIBITION GROUNDS (VÝSTAVIŠTĚ)

The extensive Exhibition Grounds in the inner suburb of Holešovice has a fine old-fashioned funfair among other attractions.

🔲 E–F2 ⊠ U Výstaviště, Holešovice ☎ 2010 3204 ⏰ Tue–Fri from 2PM; Sat–Sun from 10AM (evening opening for performances) 🍴 Cafés and restaurants 🚋 Tram 5, 12, 17 to Výstaviště 💰 Cheap

### HISTORIC TRAM RIDE

A vintage tram trundles round a circuit linking the city centre, Malá Strana and the Exhibition Grounds.

### MILITARY MUSEUM (VOJENSKÉ MUZEUM) ➤ 53

### PUPPET THEATRES ➤ 80

### ZOO (ZOOLOGICKÁ ZAHRADA)

Not the world's most outstanding zoological garden, but useful to know about and conveniently placed opposite Troja Château (➤ 48).

🔲 D1 ⊠ U Trojského zámku 3, Troja ☎ 688 04 80 ⏰ Mar–Apr daily 9–5. May daily 9–6. Jun–Sep daily 9–7. Oct–Feb daily 9–4 🍴 Buffet 🚇 Nádraží Holešovice, then Bus 112 to Zoologická zahrada 💰 Cheap

## Keeping 'em happy

There are enough jazz bands, sword-swallowers and other entertainers on the streets to keep kids happily staring for hours, not to mention any number of tall towers to climb. Incorrigible junior consumers will find their favourite soft drinks on sale, the local ice-cream is excellent and Prague is no longer a 'One-Mac-city'; the famous hamburgers are on sale at several locations and pizzas and similar snacks are available as well.

## Getting around

Tram rides are a novelty to many children – and are also an excellent way of getting to know the city. Other entertaining ways of moving around include the 'train' which chugs up to Prague Castle from Old Town Square and back, and the horse-drawn carriages, also based in Old Town Square.

# COMMUNIST MEMENTOES

## Communist corruption

Despite being lowered every evening into a refrigerated chamber and receiving the attentions of the best embalmers available, the corpse of Klement Gottwald (1896–1953, Czechoslovakia's first Communist president), in the National Memorial, continued to putrefy. When platoons of Young Pioneers were brought to admire their leader, most of what they saw was not Klement, but skilfully crafted replacement parts.

## Home sweet home

*Paneláks* (see main text) are regarded with a mixture of affection and exasperation. Any accommodation is desirable in a city with an acute housing shortage, especially if it's supplied with hot and cold running water and central heating like most *paneláks*. The downside is the dreariness of the surroundings.

### BAROLOMĚJSKÁ POLICE STATION
The police station where Václav Havel was regularly brought in for interrogation in his dissident days has now been returned to its former owners, an order of nuns, who have leased part of it as a pension. If you book far enough ahead you can spend the night in Havel's cell.
➕ E4/5 ✉ Cloister Inn, Bartolomějská 9, Staré město ☎ 232 1289 Ⓜ Národní třída ♿ Accessible only to pension guests

### HOLIDAY INN PRAGUE
A totally authentic example of the monumental wedding-cake architecture of the Stalinist era.
➕ C2 ✉ Koulova 15, Dejvice ☎ 24 39 31 11 🍴 Café and restaurant Ⓜ Dejvická 🚊 Tram 20, 25 to Podbaba ♿ Expensive to stay

### JAN PALACH'S GRAVE
The grave of the self-immolating student Jan Palach (► 43) is in the vast cemetery at Olšany. A square in the Old Town is also named after him, and flowers are regularly placed on the spot in Wenceslas Square where he died.
➕ H–J5 ✉ Olšanské hřbitovy (Olšany cemetery), Vinohradská 🕐 Daily 8–7 Ⓜ Flóra or Želivského ♿ Free

### MEMORIAL TO 17 NOVEMBER 1989
In an arcade on Národní třída, a little memorial panel of hands raised in supplication marks the place where 50,000 student demonstrators were attacked by riot police – an event seen as the genesis of the Velvet Revolution.
➕ E5 ✉ Národní třída 16, Nové město Ⓜ Národní třída ♿ Free

### THE METRO
Prague's immaculate Metro once sported a number of fine examples of Socialist-Realist art, of which the only one remaining is the mosaic of a chisel-chinned worker and his mate at Anděl station.
➕ D6 🕐 5AM–midnight Ⓜ Anděl

### NATIONAL MEMORIAL (NÁRODNÍ PAMÁTNÍK)
Built in the interwar period, this great slab of a building atop the steep rise to the east of the city centre served as a shrine to prominent Communist Party men. The Memorial's future is uncertain.
➕ G4 ✉ U památníku, Žižkov, Prague 3 Ⓜ Florenc then uphill walk 🚌 Bus 133, 207

### PANELÁKS
All around the outskirts of Prague are the monolithic housing estates composed of high-rise blocks nicknamed *paneláks*, system-built on the Soviet model from concrete panels manufactured on site.

# PRAGUE
## *where to...*

# CZECH CUISINE

## Prices

Expect to pay for dinner per person without drinks:

£££ over Kč600

££ Kč200–600

£ Kč100–200

## Dumplings

Love them or leave them, *knedlíky* (dumplings) are the inevitable accompaniment to much Czech cooking, adding further solidity to an already substantial cuisine. Every housewife has her prized recipe, using bread, flour, potatoes or semolina, and the home-made *knedlík* may have a lightness often absent from a restaurant's offering.

### DERBY (£)

Excellent value includes basic soup and sandwich lunch for just a few crowns.

✚ F2 ✉ Dukelských hrdinů 20 🚋 Tram 5, 12, 17 to Veletržní

### FREGATA (££)

An alternative to the Vltava (➤ 63) for traditional fish dishes.

✚ E6 ✉ Ladova 3 ☎ 29 31 21 Ⓜ Karlovo náměstí

### MALOSTRANSKÁ BESEDA (£)

Czech food served in Malá Strana Square.

✚ D4 ✉ Malostranské náměstí ☎ 53 55 28 Ⓜ Malostranská

### MYSLIVNA (££)

Improbably located in a backstreet in suburban Vinohrady, this restaurant ('The Hunter's Lodge') is worth seeking out for its delicious game specialities.

✚ G5 ✉ Jagellonská 21, Vinohrady ☎ 627 02 09 Ⓜ Jiřího z Poděbrad

### NA OŘECHOVCE (££)

Pub-restaurant with some of the city's best Czech food, deep in the garden suburb of Ořechovce ('Walnut Grove').

✚ B3 ✉ Východní 7, Dejvice ☎ 312 48 42 🚋 Tram 1, 2, 18 to Sibeliova

### NA RYBÁRNĚ (££)

Fishy delights in a restaurant supposedly once frequented by President Havel.

✚ E5/6 ✉ Gorazdova 17, Nové město ☎ 29 97 95 Ⓜ Karlovo náměstí

### PLZEŇSKÁ RESTAURACE (££)

In the basement of the beautifully restored Municipal House (➤ 46) is this art-nouveau designer's idea of what a Bohemian beer hall should look like.

✚ E/F4 ✉ Náměstí Republiky 5, Staré město ☎ 2200 2763 Ⓜ Náměstí Republiky

### POD KŘÍDLEM (£££)

Smart surroundings and impeccable food. Also conveniently close to the National Theatre.

✚ E5 ✉ Národní třída 10, Nové město ☎ 24 91 23 77 Ⓜ Národní třída

### RESTAURACE NA POŘÍČÍ (£)

An unpretentious but well-run corner restaurant frequented mostly by locals but happy to welcome tourists. Close to Masaryk Station and the Municipal House.

✚ F4 ✉ Na poříčí 20, Nové město ☎ 2481 1363 Ⓜ Náměstí Republiky

### RESTAURANT KRÁLE JIŘÍHO (£)

A useful port of call if you find yourself in suburban Vinohrady.

✚ G5 ✉ Slavíkova 6 ☎ 627 29 69 Ⓜ Jiřího z Poděbrad

### STARÁ RADNICE (££)

A handy lunch-stop along the Hradčany tourist trail.

✚ C4 ✉ Loretánská 1, Hradčany ☎ 2051 1140 🚋 Tram 22 to Pražský hrad or Pohořelec

### U BENEDIKTA (££)

Conventional Czech cooking done with more

than the usual degree of sophistication, and served in a patio tucked away behind the big Kotva department store.

✚ E4 ✉ Benediktská 11, Staré město ☎ 2481 3872 Ⓜ Náměstí Republiky

### U ČIŽKŮ (££)
Attractive Old Bohemian farmhouse atmosphere with meaty specialities to match, such as a platter of duck, pork and sausage with dumplings and sauerkraut for light relief.

✚ E5 ✉ Karlovo náměstí 34, Nové město ☎ 29 88 91 Ⓜ Karlovo náměstí

### U KALICHA (£££)
Thanks to the Good Soldier Švejk's patronage in Austro-Hungarian days, this is a popular place with visitors from abroad familiar with the famous Czech anti-hero. Solid food among much Švejkian memorabilia.

✚ E/F5/6 ✉ Na bojišti 12–14, Nové město ☎ 29 07 01 or 29 19 45 Ⓜ I P Pavlova

### U MATOUŠE (£)
Traditional dishes plus innovative but still authentic explorations into what Czech (and Moravian) cuisine is all about. Give 24 hours notice if you want to feast on roast duckling cooked as it really should be.

✚ D5 ✉ Preslova 17, Smíchov ☎ 54 62 84 or 54 18 77 Ⓜ Anděl

### U MĚSTSKÉ KNIHOVNY (£)
A fine place for solid local food served in a relaxed atmosphere.

✚ E4 ✉ Valentinská 11, Staré město ☎ 232 17 16 or 231 08 67 Ⓜ Staroměstská

### U MIKULÁŠE DAČICKÉHO (££)
Set designers from the famous Barrandov film studios fitted out this restaurant as a medieval banqueting hall in the 1920s. It provides an atmospheric setting for the hearty food.

✚ D5 ✉ Viktora Huga 2, Smíchov ☎ 54 93 12 Ⓒ Closed Sun Ⓜ Anděl

### U PASTÝŘKY (££)
The rustic surroundings of a log cabin with a big open fireplace at 'The Little Shepherdess' are an alternative to the Pezinok (➤ 62) if you wish to sample Slovak cooking.

✚ F5/6 ✉ Bělehradská 15, Nusle ☎ 691 35 55 Ⓜ I P Pavlova 🚋 Tram 11

### U PLEBÁNA (££)
Before 1989 'The Plebeian' was ironically the preserve of Communist Party bigwigs and their guests. Patrons now tend to be local and foreign business folk enjoying such delights as juicy duckling and succulent mixed grills.

✚ E4 ✉ Betlémské náměstí 10, Staré město ☎ 24 22 90 23 Ⓜ Národní třída

### VLTAVA (£)
Good-value soup, carp and trout served close to the Vltava (from which one hopes the ingredients have not been fished).

✚ E5 ✉ Rašínovo nábřeží, Nové město ☎ 29 49 64 Ⓜ Karlovo náměstí

### Alive, alive o!
Cut off from the sea, Czechs have traditionally made much of freshwater fish such as trout and carp. The huge ponds constructed in the Middle Ages in which the carp in particular were bred in their countless thousands are still very much in use today. Carp make up the traditional Christmas Eve dinner, and are bought live by sharp-eyed buyers from the equally sharp dealers who set up fish tanks in the streets and squares in the days leading up to the festival.

# INTERNATIONAL CUISINE

## CONTINENTAL

### CERBERUS (££)
Attractive setting for a *mélange* of Czech and international cooking. Situated in the New Town, not far from the Municipal House.
F4 ✉ Soukenická 19, Nové město ☎ 23 10 985 Ⓜ Náměstí Republiky

### DAVID (££)
An intimate setting and faultless food, including melt-in-the-mouth lamb, a house speciality.
D4 ✉ Tržiště 21, Malá Strana ☎ 53 93 25 Ⓜ Malostranská 🚋 Tram 22 to Malostranské náměstí

### FROM THE NEW WORLD (££)
On the upper floor of the city's first Western-style shopping mall in the inner suburb of Vinohrady.
G5 ✉ Vinohradská 50 ☎ 2209 7320 Ⓜ Naměsti miru

### HANAVSKÝ PAVILON (££)
The delightful little art-nouveau Hanava Pavilion, perched high above the Vltava, serves fine food for its mostly foreign guests.
D3 ✉ Letenské sady 173 ☎ 32 57 92 🚋 Tram 18 to Chotkovy sady

### KAMPA PARK (££)
Stylish food served in a pretty pink house on Kampa Island.
D4 ✉ Na Kampě 8b ☎ 5731 3493 Ⓜ Malostranská 🚋 Tram 22 to Malostranské náměstí

### KLÁŠTERNÍ VINÁRNA (££)
Excellent steaks in the 'Monastery' wine restaurant.
E5 ✉ Národní třída 8, Nové město ☎ 29 05 96 Ⓜ Národní třída

### LOBKOVICKÁ VINÁRNA (££)
Imaginative international cooking in a wine restaurant run by the aristocratic Lobkovic family. Features wines from their estate at Mělník.
C4 ✉ Vlašská 17, Malá Strana ☎ 53 01 85 🚋 Tram 22 to Malostranské náměstí

### SVATÁ KLÁRA (££)
Charcoal-grilled and flambéed specialities in the aristocratic ambience of Troja Château.
D1 ✉ U trojského zámku 9 ☎ 688 04 05 Ⓜ Nádraží Holešovice then Bus 112 to Zoologická zahrada

### U MODRÉ KACHNIČKY (££)
'The Blue Duckling' was an instant success when it opened in 1993. First-rate game features among a range of dishes, served in a setting of intimate, antiques-furnished rooms.
D4 ✉ Nebovidská 6, Malá Strana ☎ 5732 0308 🚋 Tram 22 to Hellichova

### U MODRÉ RŮŽE (££)
In an atmospheric Old Town cellar, 'The Blue Rose' serves fine fish and game.
E4 ✉ Rytířská 16, Staré město ☎ 26 10 81 or 26 38 86 Ⓜ Můstek

## Diners beware
Since 1989, restaurants targeted at a specifically foreign clientele have multiplied in number. The temptation has been to charge international prices without providing a corresponding level of nutrition, sophistication or service. Bills should always be checked and a tip given only if service has been satisfactory.

## U ZLATÉ HRUŠKY (£££)

The 'Golden Pear', in a charming rococo house in romantic Nový svět, has an attractive outdoor section opposite.

➕ C4 ✉ Nový svět 3, Hradčany ☎ 53 11 33
🚋 Tram 22 to Brusnice

## V ZÁTIŠÍ (££)

All-round excellence in a sophisticated ambience just off the Royal Way. This fine restaurant (whose name means 'Still Life' or 'Seclusion') opened not long after the 1989 Velvet Revolution and has since become a Prague institution.

➕ E4 ✉ Liliová 1, Staré město ☎ 24 22 89 77
🚇 Staroměstská

## GRILLS

### OPERA GRILL (£££)

Fabulous food served in an intimate setting.

➕ E4 ✉ Karoliny Světlé 35, Staré město ☎ 26 55 08
🚇 Národní třída

### ROTISSERIE (££)

Long-established grill which has maintained its reputation in the face of much competition.

➕ E5 ✉ Mikulandská 6, Nové město ☎ 24 91 23 34
🚇 Národní třída

## SEAFOOD

### CANADIAN LOBSTER (£££)

Expect to pay high prices for the impeccable fish dishes.

➕ E4 ✉ Husova 15, Staré město ☎ 24 21 35 30
🚇 Národní třída or Staroměstská

## REYKAVÍK (££)

A welcome stop along the tourist trail between Old Town Square and Charles Bridge, this Icelandic restaurant serves fresh fish flown in from the cold waters of the North Atlantic.

➕ E4 ✉ Karlova 20, Staré město ☎ 2422 9251
🚇 Staroměstská

## U VOJÁČKŮ (££)

Good fish soups and salmon steaks not far from the Vltava in left-bank Prague.

➕ D5 ✉ Vodní 11
☎ 53 56 68 🚋 Trams 6, 9 to Kinského zahrada

## AMERICAN

### AVALON (£££)

Convincing replica of an American diner set in Malá Strana Square.

➕ D4 ✉ Malostranské náměstí 12, Malá Strana ☎ 5753 0021
🚇 Malostranská 🚋 Tram 22 to Malostranské náměstí

### BUFFALO BILL'S (£–££)

A far cry from Middle European fare: tacos, tortilla soup and other Tex-Mex delicacies.

➕ E5 ✉ Vodičkova 9 ☎ 2421 5479 🚇 Můstek

## FRENCH

### LA PROVENCE (£££)

French specialities, from cassoulet to coq au vin.

➕ E4 ✉ Štupartská 9, Staré město ☎ 232 48 01
🚇 Náměstí Republiky

### U MALÍŘŮ (£££)

'The Painter' serves sublime French food, in

## Local fast food

Western fast food is now available in many places, but better by far (and much cheaper) for a quick snack are the local *obložené chlebíčky* (open sandwiches). Each of these is a miniature meal in itself, perhaps consisting of a sliver or two of ham or salami and a slice of hard-boiled egg, the whole garnished with mayonnaise and topped with pieces of gherkin and red pepper.

an ancient house in the middle of Malá Strana.

🕂 D4 🖂 Maltézské náměstí 11, Malá Strana ☎ 5732 0317
🚊 Tram 22, 23 to Hellichova

## ITALIAN

### BELLA NAPOLI (£–££)

Not just Neapolitan food but other Italian delights on offer only a short step from Wenceslas Square.

🕂 E5 🖂 V jámě 8, Nové město ☎ 24 22 73 15
🚇 Muzeum

### IL RITROVO (£–££)

An amiable Florentine restaurant not far from Wenceslas Square, designed to make Italian expats feel *a casa*.

🕂 F5/6 🖂 Lublaňská 11, Vinohrady ☎ 29 65 29
🚇 I P Pavlova

### SEGAFREDO ESPRESSO AND TRATTORIA (££)

Italian excitement in the old Severin Palace.

🕂 E4 🖂 Na příkopě 10, Nové město ☎ 24 21 07 16
🚇 Můstek or Náměstí Republiky

## GREEK

### FAROS (£–££)

Moussaka and other Greek specialities transport you to a sun-soaked world far beyond the confines of backstreet Malá Strana.

🕂 C4 🖂 Šporkova 5, Malá Strana ☎ 5731 6945 🚊 Tram 22 to Malostranské náměstí

## MIDDLE EASTERN

### ADONIS (£)

An extremely popular lunch spot offering a

whole range of Middle Eastern delicacies.

🕂 E5 🖂 Jungmannova 21, Nové město ☎ 268 908
🚇 Můstek or Národní třída

### FAKHRELDINE (££)

Authentic Lebanese food from a branch of this internationally famous restaurant group.

🕂 F3/4 🖂 Klimentská 48, Nové město ☎ 23 27 970
🚇 Florenc 🚊 Tram 3 to Těšnov

## ASIAN

### ASIE (£–££)

Tasty exceptions to the sometimes bland offerings of some of Prague's 'Chinese' restaurants make it worth the trip out to Asie.

🕂 G4 🖂 Seifertova 18, Žižkov ☎ 697 6610 🚊 Tram 5, 9, 26 to Lipanská

### PRAHA TAMURA (£££)

An excellent Japanese restaurant in the heart of Prague's Old Town.

🕂 E4 🖂 Havelská 6, Staré město ☎ 24 23 20 56
🚇 Můstek

### SATÉ (£)

Before 1989, no Czech porker expected to end up as *satay* on a skewer, but Indonesian eating has now colonised this square in upper Hradčany.

🕂 C4 🖂 Pohořelec 152/3, Hradčany ☎ 53 21 13
🚊 Tram 22 to Pohořelec

### U ZLATÉHO HADA (££)

Once a café, the venerable 'Golden Snake' is now better known for its Chinese cuisine.

🕂 E4 🖂 Karlova 18, Staré město ☎ 24 22 08 43
🚇 Staroměstská

## Czech wines and spirits

Although little known abroad Czech wines are surprisingly good, especially both reds and whites from Moravia, and make an interesting (albeit temporary) souvenir. Spirits are cheap and often excellent. Slivovice (plum brandy) is well known, a supposed cure for all ills, while Becherovka, prepared in Carlsbad to a secret recipe, has a unique and pungent flavour.

# VEGETARIAN & SCENIC RESTAURANTS

## VEGETARIAN

### COUNTRY LIFE (£)
Healthy eating at a couple of central venues.
➕ E5 ✉ Jungmannova 1, Nové město ☎ 24 19 17 39 Ⓜ Národní třída or Můstek

### GOVINDA VEGETARIAN CLUB (£)
An alternative Hare Krishna establishment to the U Govindy (see below), in a convenient location not far from the Municipal House (➤ 46).
➕ F4 ✉ Soukenicka 27, Nové město ☎ 2481 6016 Ⓜ Náměstí Republicky

### RADOST CAFÉ FX (£)
Trendy café for the chic and cool.
➕ F6 ✉ Bělehradská 120, Vinohrady ☎ 25 12 10 Ⓜ I P Pavlova

### U GOVINDY
A Hare Krishna eating-place, in the unlikely surroundings of the city's eastern suburbs. As much wholefood as you can digest. Pay by making a donation.
➕ J2 ✉ Na hrázi 5, Palmovka ☎ 2481 6016 Ⓜ Palmovka

## RESTAURANTS WITH A VIEW OR TERRACE

### NA ZVONAŘCE (£)
Billiards and bulky Czech food with a fine view of the slopes that were once covered with the vineyards that gave Vinohrady its name.
➕ F6 ✉ Šafaříkova 1, Vinohrady ☎ 2425 2775 🚊 Tram 6, 11 to Pod Karlovem or Nuselské schody

### NEBOZÍZEK (££)
The 'Little Auger' looks the other way from the Parnas (see below), ie from the slopes of Petřín Hill towards the centre. Reached by funicular.
➕ C5 ✉ Petřínské sady 411, Malá Strana ☎ 53 79 05 🚠 Funicular

### PARNAS (£££)
For that special night out. Sumptuous turn-of-the-century setting and sophisticated cuisine combined with an unbeatable view of the Vltava and Prague Castle (as long as you reserve a window table).
➕ D5 ✉ Smetanovo nábřeži 2, Staré město ☎ 2421 1901 Ⓜ Národní třída

### RESTAURACE NA VYŠEHRADĚ (£)
With its terrace and straightforward Czech cooking, this is a good place to cool off after visiting Prague's second citadel.
➕ E7 ✉ Štulcova 2, Vyšehrad ☎ 24 23 92 97 Ⓜ Vyšehrad

### U KRISTIANA (££)
Unmemorable food but a prospect to die for. 'Christians' is aboard a barge anchored off the quayside below the Smetana Embankment, with views across the Vltava to Charles Bridge, Malá Strana and Prague Castle.
➕ D4 ✉ Smetanovo nábřezi, Staré město ☎ 90 00 06 01/90 00 06 39 🚊 Tram 17, 18 to Karlovy lázně, or 6, 9, 21, 22 to Národní divadlo

## Veggie revolution
Before 1989, vegetarians venturing to Prague were liable to be served endless omelettes, perhaps with extra dumplings. Czechs still like their rich and hearty meat-based dishes, but waiters and others are no longer fazed when a foreigner expresses an interest in something else.

## Kosher food
Reliable kosher food can be had at Kosher Restaurant Shalom (£–££), in the former meeting room of the Jewish Town Hall.
➕ E4 ✉ Maislova 18, Staré město ☎ 24 81 09 29 Ⓜ Staroměstská

# PUBS, BARS & CAFÉS

## Czech beer

Lager beer was virtually invented in Bohemia, when the citizens of Pilsen (Plzeň) got together to form the 'Burghers' Brewery' in 1842 and began producing the light and tasty liquid which has spawned endless imitation 'pils' ever since but which has never been surpassed. But other Czech beers are just as good, better from the barrel than the bottle. Try Prague's own Staropramen or Braník, or the milder Budvar from České Budějovice (Budweis) in southern Bohemia.

### PUBS

#### BRANICKÁ FORMANKA
The suburban Braník brewery is one of four major breweries in Prague. This pub is its city-centre outlet.
🚇 E5 ✉ Vodičkova 26, Nové město ☎ 2421 7103 Ⓜ Můstek

#### ČERNÝ PIVOVAR
The 'Black Brewery' pumps are constantly at work pulling up the dark beer for the crowds in this no-frills Charles Square establishment.
🚇 E5 ✉ Karlovo náměstí 15, Nové město Ⓜ Karlovo náměstí

#### JAMES JOYCE
Should you ever tire of the wonders of Czech beer, here's one of the few places that offer an alternative: in this case Guinness and other Irish beers (to a largely expat crowd).
🚇 E4 ✉ Liliová 10, Staré město Ⓜ Staroměstská

#### NOVOMĚSTSKÝ PIVOVAR
The 'New Town Brewery' is Prague's other boutique brewery (after U Fleků), and is housed in a medieval building.
🚇 E5 ✉ Vodičkova 20, Nové město Ⓜ Můstek

#### U FLEKŮ
Every visitor should sup the dark and tasty beer which has been brewed on these premises for 200 years, and which is served in the raucous interior or – more congenial – in a big beer garden.

🚇 E5 ✉ Křemencova 11, Nové město ☎ 24 91 51 18 Ⓜ Karlovo náměstí or Národní třída

#### U KOCOURA
The famous old 'Tomcat' welcomes thirsty tourists making the hard trek up from Malá Strana to Prague Castle.
🚇 D4 ✉ Nerudova 2, Malá Strana 🚋 Tram 22 to Malostranské náměstí

#### U MEDVÍDKŮ
Budvar, from České Budějovice in southern Bohemia, is probably the best-known Bohemian beer apart from Pilsener. Try it here on draught – out in the garden in summer.
🚇 E4 ✉ Na Perštýně 7, Staré město Ⓜ Národní třída

#### U SVATÉHO TOMÁŠE
The monks no longer brew their own here, but the medieval ambience of St Thomas's makes it a popular stop with tour groups, who also enjoy the folk-music performances.
🚇 D4 ✉ Letenská 12, Malá Strana Ⓜ Malostranská

#### U VEJVODŮ
Don't be put off by the scruffy appearance; this is one of the most ancient and authentic of Prague's city-centre pubs, with local Staropramen on tap.
🚇 E4 ✉ Jilská 4, Staré město ☎ 24 21 05 91 Ⓜ Národní třída

#### U ZLATÉHO TYGRA
The perfect Pilsener, drawn straight from the 13th-century cellars of the 'Golden Tiger', has long

made this pub a favourite
with serious local drinkers
who remain unimpressed
by visitors, even when
they turn out to be the
president of the United
States.

🟥 E4 ✉ Husova 17, Staré
město ☎ 24 22 90 20
🚇 Staroměstská

## CAFÉS & BARS

### ARCHA

This café, situated next
to one of the country's
biggest publishing houses,
attracts a youthful,
intellectual set.

🟥 F4 ✉ Na poříčí 26, north
Nové město ☎ 232 41 49
🚇 Náměstí Republiky

### CAFÉ MILENA

Another elegant café in
Old Town Square.

🟥 E4 ✉ Staroměstské náměstí
22, Staré město ☎ 26 08 43
🚇 Staroměstská

### CAFÉ SAVOY

Turn-of-the-century
elegance in a refined café
at the Malá Strana end of
the Legions' Bridge (Most
legií).

🟥 D5 ✉ Vítězná 5, Malá
Strana ☎ 53 50 00 🚋 Tram
6, 9, 22 to Újezd

### CAFFÉ DANTE

Clean-cut Italian café
opposite the modern art
collections of the Trades
Fair Palace.

🟥 F3 ✉ Dukelských hrdinů
16, Holešovice ☎ 87 01 93
🚋 Tram 5, 12, 17 to Veletržní

### DOLCE VITA

Authentic espresso close
to Old Town Square.

🟥 E4 ✉ Široká 15, Staré
město 🚇 Staroměstská

### EVROPA

In spite of the arrogance
of charging an entrance
fee, the art-nouveau café
of the Evropa Hotel is an
experience not to be
missed.

🟥 E5 ✉ Václavské náměstí
25, Nové město ☎ 24 22 81 17
🚇 Můstek

### GULU GULU

You'll be lucky to get a
table at this trendy locale
in Bethlehem Square,
which buzzes like a
beehive until midnight.

🟥 E4 ✉ Betlémské náměstí 8,
Staré město ☎ 9001 25811
🚇 Národní třída

### INSTITUT FRANÇAIS

Pleasant French-style café
in the New Town just off
Wenceslas Square.

🟥 E5 ✉ Štěpánská 35, Nové
město ☎ 24 21 40 32
🚇 Můstek or Muzeum

### SLAVIA

This classic Central
European café, with its
view over the Vltava, is
open again after a long
and controversial period
of closure.

🟥 D5 ✉ Smetanovo nábřeží
2, Staré město ☎ 2422 0957
🚇 Národní třída

### VELRYBA

The 'Whale' opens wide
its jaws to accommodate
its clientele of trendies.

🟥 E5 ✉ Opatovická 24,
Nové město ☎ 2491 2484
🚇 Národní třída

## Turkish coffee

Espresso, cappuccino and most other kinds of coffee can now be found in Prague, but don't be surprised if you get served a traditional *turecká káva*. This is Turkish coffee, fine when you're accustomed to it and know when to stop swallowing – that is before you disturb the deposit of coffee grounds at the bottom of the cup.

# BOOKS & ANTIQUES

## Bargains... perhaps

Czechs are great readers, and until recently new and second-hand books were extremely cheap, many of them in languages other than Czech. Prices have risen considerably since 1989, but there are still many bargains. That said, prices for antique books are now well in line with those on the international market.

## NEW BOOKS

### ALBATROS
Specialises in children's books, an area of publishing in which Czech authors and illustrators have long excelled.
➕ E4 ✉ Havelská 20, Staré město ☎ 2422 9322
Ⓜ Můstek

### CIZOJAZYČNÁ LITERATURA
Has fair-sized stocks of what its name ('Foreign-language Literature') implies and much else besides.
➕ E4 ✉ Na příkopě 27, Staré město ☎ 26 28 37 Ⓜ Můstek

### FRANZ KAFKA
An excellent range of both new and second-hand books, mostly in German.
➕ D4 ✉ U lužického semináře 19, Malá Strana ☎ 53 15 52
Ⓜ Malostranská

### THE GLOBE BOOKSTORE AND COFFEEHOUSE
A congenial home-from-home for US expats and anyone hungry for all kinds of literature in English, as well as bagels and American-style coffee. The Globe is located in the inner-city suburb of Holešovice, on the north bank of the Vltava, but is easy to reach by public transport.
➕ F2 ✉ Janovského 14, near Strossmayerovo náměstí, Holešovice ☎ 66 71 26 10
🚋 Tram 5, 12, 17 to Strossmayerovo náměstí

### KANZELSBERGER
Good selection of new titles, including children's stories and books on Prague and the Czech Republic, many in languages other than Czech.
➕ E5 ✉ Václavské náměstí (Wenceslas Square) 42, Nové město. ☎ 24 21 73 35
Ⓜ Můstek

### KIWI
Don't be put off by the travel agency on the ground floor; the shop in the basement has one of the best selections of maps and guides in town. Small second-hand section.
➕ E5 ✉ Jungmannova 23, Nové město ☎ 2423 4756
Ⓜ Národní třída

### KNIHKUPECTVÍ NA MŮSTKU
A famous-name bookstore with an excellent selection of maps.
➕ E4 ✉ Na příkopě 3, Staré město ☎ 2421 6383
Ⓜ Můstek

### KNIHKUPECTVÍ U ČERNÉ MATKY BOŽÍ
A large, well-stocked bookshop that carries virtually every foreign-language title published locally, as well as a good range of travel books and maps. Unmissable location in the Cubist House at the Black Madonna (▶ 56).
➕ E4 ✉ Celetná 34, Staré město ☎ 2421 1155
Ⓜ Náměstí Republicky

### U KNIHOMOLA
An enticing new basement bookshop, 'The Bookworm' attempts to supply the fullest possible range of foreign-language volumes. It has the bonus of an even deeper

basement café with periodicals to read.
🔲 G5 ✉ Mánesova 79, Vinohrady ☎ 627 7770 Ⓜ Jiřího z Poděbrad

## ANTIQUES & ANTIQUARIAN BOOKSHOPS

### ANTIKVARIÁT EVA KOZÁKOVÁ

Old photographs, prints and postcards plus innumerable old (mostly Czech) books.
🔲 E5 ✉ Myslíkova 10, Nové město ☎ 29 44 02 Ⓜ Karlovo náměstí

### ANTIKVARIÁT GALERIE MŮSTEK

Printed treasures of all kinds in a spacious Old Town basement, including many engravings, maps and even paintings.
🔲 E4 ✉ 28 října 13, Staré město ☎ 26 80 58 Ⓜ Můstek

### ANTIKVARIÁT KAREL KŘENEK

Refined establishment near the start of the Royal Way, with an excellent range of prints and watercolours as well as fine old books.
🔲 E4 ✉ Celetná 31, Staré město ☎ 231 47 34 Ⓜ Náměstí Republiky

### ANTIKVARIÁT NA VALDŠTEJNSKÉM NÁMĚSTÍ

The Malá Strana mecca for lovers of old books.
🔲 D4 ✉ Valdštejnské náměstí 7, Malá Strana Ⓜ Malostranská

### ANTIKVARIÁT U KARLOVA MOSTU

Fine old books and printed memorabilia of all kinds. Not particularly cheap.
🔲 E4 ✉ Karlova 2, Staré město ☎ 24 22 92 05 Ⓜ Staroměstská

### DOROTHEUM

This branch of the long-established Vienna auction-house has a fine range of antiques of all kinds. No bargains, but no rip-offs either.
🔲 E4 ✉ Ovocný trh 2, Staré město ☎ 24 22 20 01 Ⓜ Můstek or Náměstí Republicky

### GALERIE LUKAS

Exquisite objects of international as well as Czech origin.
🔲 E5 ✉ Národní třída 21, Nové město ☎ 24 21 33 38 Ⓜ Národní třída

### PRAŽSKÉ STAROŽITNOSTI

'Prague Antiques' sells jewellery, porcelain and paintings galore.
🔲 E5 ✉ Mikulandská 8, Nové město ☎ 29 41 70 Ⓜ Národní třída

### VLADIMIR ANDRLE

This antique shop, in Wenceslas Square, is a handy starting point for your hunt for collectables.
🔲 E5 ✉ Václavské náměstí 17, Nové město ☎ 2400 9166 Ⓜ Můstek

### ZLATÁ KORUNA

Antique coins, medals and paper money.
🔲 E4 ✉ Pařížská 8, Staré město ☎ 231 32 85 Ⓜ Staroměstská

## Wenceslas Hollar

One of the first artists to make accurate drawings of the English landscape was Wenceslas Hollar. Born in 1607 in Bohemia, Václav (to give him his Czech name) sought refuge abroad following the Protestant defeat at the Battle of the White Mountain, and was employed as a draughtsman by the Earl of Arundel. A trawl through Prague's antiquarian bookshops might turn up a Hollar original, such as his wonderfully detailed 1636 panorama of the city, but there are plenty of alternatives by other artists – drawings, engravings and maps – at affordable prices.

# GIFTS, SOUVENIRS & MUSIC

## TOYS, PUPPETS & SOUVENIRS

### ALBATROS
The place to look for soft toys as well as children's books.
✚ E4 ✉ Havelská 20, Staré město ☎ 2422 9322 Ⓜ Můstek

### ČESKÝ NÁRODNÍ PODNIK
Folksy artefacts include Christmas cribs as well as willow whips to harass village maidens with at Eastertime.
✚ E4 ✉ Husova 12, Staré město ☎ 24 21 08 86 Ⓜ Staroměstská

### DIVADELNÍ KNIHKUPECTVÍ A LOUTKY
Looking for a puppet as a souvenir? 'Theatre Bookshop and Marionettes' sells hand-made marionettes of superior quality to those sold on the street – at correspondingly higher prices. Worth visiting if only to study the several kinds of Devil that play such a prominent part in Czech puppetry.
✚ E4 ✉ Celetná 17, Staré město Ⓜ Náměstí Republiky

### DŘEVENÉ HRAČKY
Sensible and imaginative wooden toys.
✚ E4 ✉ Karlova 26, Staré město Ⓜ Staroměstská

### EXPOZICE FRANZE KAFKY
Prague's most famous writer must have spun round in his grave many times at the souvenir industry, which has impressed his haggard features on countless T-shirts. This is the least tacky selection of Kafkeriana that is on offer in the city.
✚ E4 ✉ Corner of Maislova and Kaprova, Staré město Ⓜ Staroměstská

### KROKODIL
New and second-hand model trains galore, including Communist-era rarities.
✚ D5 ✉ Bartolomějská 3, Staré město Ⓜ Národní třída

### LIŠKA
Central Europeans still wear their furs without shame, purchased from elegant outlets such as 'The Fox' near Old Town Square. If you're on a budget, fox-fur hats at bargain prices can be found on a stall in the Havelská market.
✚ E4 ✉ Železná 1, Staré město Ⓜ Staroměstská

### MUSEUM SHOP
Unusually tasteful and original souvenirs based on the treasures of the many Prague museums, plus foreign art books not available elsewhere in Prague. An example to other souvenir shops worldwide; where else, for example, could you buy a china mug with elegant sgraffito patterning?
✚ D4 ✉ Jiřská 6, Hradčany ☎ 2437 3255 🚊 Tram 22 to Pražský hrad

### OBCHOD S LOUTKAMI
Another place to find a plethora of puppetry.
✚ C4 ✉ Nerudova 47, Malá

## Kafka at home
One of the many places lived in by Jewish novelist Franz Kafka was the house on Celetná Street adjoining Týn Church. A blank window faces down the south aisle of the church's nave from the bedroom in which Kafka slept and dreamed as a child.

## Sgraffito
The Schwarzenberg Palace on Hradčany Square is probably Prague's most splendidly sgraffitoed building. Sgraffito work involves picking out patterns in two shades of plasterwork to accentuate the architectural character of the building, or to cover the façade with lively pictures (as in the Martinic Palace, also in Hradčany Square).

Strana ▦ Tram 22 to
Malostranské náměstí

## ARTS & CRAFTS

### CRISTALLINO
Designer glassware, a
Czech speciality. Two
branches.
✚ E4 ✉ Celetná 12, Staré
město ☎ 24 21 48 52
Ⓜ Náměstí Republiky.
Also at
✚ E4 ✉ Celetná 19, Staré
město ☎ 26 12 65
Ⓜ Náměstí Republiky

### CRYSTAL
Wonderfully decorated
glass from Nový Bor in
northern Bohemia.
✚ E4 ✉ Karlova 21, 24, Staré
město ☎ 25 46 25
Ⓜ Staroměstská

### GALERIE DOMINO
Czech and Slovak applied
arts.
✚ C3 ✉ Wuchterlova 14,
Dejvice ☎ 2431 7659
Ⓜ Dejvická

### GALERIE PEITHNER-LICHTENFELS
Modern Czech (and
Austrian) art, including
works from the inter-war
period.
✚ E4 ✉ Michalská 12, Staré
město ☎ 24 22 76 80
Ⓜ Můstek

### GRANÁT
Bohemian garnets are
world-famous; this shop
has the most varied
selection.
✚ E4 ✉ Dlouhá 30, Staré
město ☎ 231 5612
Ⓜ Náměstí Republicky

### MOSER
The outlet for the fine
crystal and porcelain made
in Carlsbad (Karlovy vary),
plus porcelain from
Meissen and Herend.
✚ E4 ✉ Na příkopě 12, Staré
město ☎ 24 21 12 93 .
Ⓜ Můstek or Náměstí Republiky

### SKLO BOHEMIA
Bohemian glassware from
Světlá nad Sázavou.
✚ E4 ✉ Na příkopě 17, Staré
město ☎ 24 21 05 74
Ⓜ Můstek or Náměstí
Republiky

## MUSIC

### AGHARTA
Jazz, jazz and more jazz on
sale at this nightspot.
✚ F5 ✉ Krakovská 5, Nové
město 🕐 Evenings only
Ⓜ Muzeum

### BONTONLAND KORUNA
Reputedly the biggest
music store in Central
Europe, although better
for pop and rock than
classical music. Also has a
full range of videos. In the
labyrinthine basement of
the Koruna Palace at the
corner of Wenceslas
Square and Na Příkopě.
✚ E4 ✉ Václavské náměstí 1,
Nové město ☎ 2423 5356
Ⓜ Můstek

### POPRON
CDs and tapes galore.
✚ E5 ✉ Jungmannova 30,
Nové město Ⓜ Národní třída or
Můstek

## Musical miscellany
In addition to excellent discs of
music by the classical composers
most closely associated with the
city (Mozart, Dvořák,
Smetana...), Prague offers
strongly flavoured and highly
individual pop music (Šum
Svistu, or Laura and her Tigers,
Support Lesbiens, Shalom...).
Even more distinctive are the
brass bands — the best you've
ever heard — pumping out Czech
(yes, Czech) old-time favourites
such as Roll Out The Barrel
(Škoda lásky).

# DEPARTMENT STORES, MARKETS & FOOD

## DEPARTMENT STORES

### Red Army surplus

After 1989, the Warsaw Pact crumbled and the Red Army began its long retreat back to Moscow, shedding its surplus equipment as it went. Many Czech farmers now sport a Kalashnikov rather than a humble shotgun, while visitors may still find themselves tempted by the trim greatcoats or improbably high-peaked officers' caps on sale wherever tourists congregate.

### BÍLÁ LABUŤ

The 'White Swan' is a long-established department store on an unfashionable but interesting shopping street just to the east of the Old Town (a smaller branch is now open on Wenceslas Square opposite the National Museum).

⊞ F4 ✉ Na Poříčí 23, north Nové město 🚇 Náměstí Republiky

### KOTVA

The 'Anchor' store was completed in 1975 and for a while was the city's foremost shopping mecca, though the range of goods would have seemed pretty basic to Western consumers. Nowadays it is full of fine things from all over the world, though the anodised aluminium and tinted glass exterior remains as intimidating as ever.

⊞ E4 ✉ Náměstí Republiky 8, Staré město 🚇 Náměstí Republiky

### KRONE

A Germanic equivalent of Tesco, on Wenceslas Square.

⊞ E4 ✉ Václavské náměstí 21 🚇 Můstek

### TESCO

Rival to Kotva, and once bearing the impeccably proletarian name of 'Máj' (May), this department store is now in British hands. A ride up the escalator gives a good view.

⊞ E5 ✉ Národní 26, Nové město 🚇 Národní třída

## MARKETS

### HAVELSKÁ/ V KOTCÍCH

Atmospheric market for fruit and vegetables, as well as souvenirs.

⊞ E4 ✉ Staré město ⊙ Daily 🚇 Můstek

### PRAGUE MARKET

Comprehensive market on the far side of the Vltava, north of the Old Town.

⊞ G3 ✉ Bubenské nábřeží, Holešovice ⊙ Daily 🚇 Vltavská

### PRAŽSKÁ BURZA

Cheap clothes, motor parts and an abundance of things you won't want – but fascinating even so.

⊞ F2 ✉ Výstaviště (Exhibition Grounds), Holešovice ⊙ Sat–Sun 9–2 🚇 Holešovice 🚋 Tram 5, 12, 17

## FOOD SHOPS

### COUNTRY LIFE

Here are the healthy wholefoods that can otherwise be difficult to obtain in this calorie-addicted city.

⊞ E4 ✉ Melantrichova 15, Staré město 🚇 Můstek

### FRUITS DE FRANCE

'French Fruits' changed the face of food shopping in Prague not long after the Velvet Revolution, and is still the place for classy imported foods.

⊞ E4 ✉ Jindřišská 9, Nové město 🚇 Můstek

### UZENINY

Every kind of Central European sausage.

⊞ E5 ✉ Václavské náměstí 34 🚇 Můstek

# OPERA & CLASSICAL MUSIC

## OPERA

### ESTATES THEATRE (STAVOVSKÉ DIVADLO)

The venue that saw the première of Mozart's *Don Giovanni* in 1787 has been restored to its pristine neoclassical glory. Regular performances of Wolfgang's greatest hits.

➕ E4 ✉ Ovocný trh, Staré město ☎ 24 21 50 01 or 26 77 97 Ⓜ Můstek

### NATIONAL THEATRE (NÁRODNÍ DIVADLO)

Operas from both the Czech and international repertoire in a sumptuous setting.

➤ 36

### STATE OPERA

Opened in 1887 as the Deutsches Theater (German Theatre), this neo-Renaissance building became the Smetana Theatre (Smetanovo divadlo) after World War II. It's now the home of the State Opera, with performances from the international repertoire and classical ballet.

➕ F5 ✉ Wilsonova 4, Nové město ☎ 24 22 76 93. Box office: 26 53 53 Ⓜ Muzeum

## CLASSICAL MUSIC

### BERTRAMKA

The villa of Mozart's Prague patrons is now a museum and chamber concert venue.

➤ 57

### HOUSE AT THE STONE BELL (DŮM U KAMMENÉHO ZVONU)

Contemporary classical compositions augment the traditional repertoire in this Gothic mansion on Old Town Square.

➕ E4 ✉ Staroměstské náměstí 13, Staré město ☎ 2482 7526 Ⓜ Staroměstská

### KLEMENTINUM

Chamber concerts in the Hall of Mirrors (Zrcadlová síň) of this vast complex.

➕ E4 ✉ Křižovnické náměstí, Staré město ☎ 2422 9500 Ⓜ Staroměstská

### LIECHTENSTEIN PALACE (LICHTENSTEJNSKÝ PALÁC)

Palatial setting for symphonic and other perfomances.

➕ D4 ✉ Malostranské náměstí 13, Malá Strana ☎ 53 09 43 Ⓜ Staroměstská 🚋 Tram 22 to Malostranské náměstí

### LOBKOVIC PALACE (LOBKOVICKÝ PALÁC)

Chamber concerts in the banqueting hall of this palace in Prague Castle precinct.

➕ D4 ✉ Jiřská 3, Hradčany ☎ 53 73 06 Ⓜ Malostranská then uphill walk 🚋 Tram 22 to Pražský hrad

### NOSTIC PALACE (NOSTICKÝ PALÁC)

Count Nostic was the founder of the Estates Theatre. His own palace makes a fine setting for chamber concerts.

➕ D4 ✉ Maltézské náměstí 1, Malá Strana ☎ 5731 1590 🚋 Tram 22 to Hellichova

### RUDOLFINUM

This splendid neo-Renaissance pile on the banks of the Vltava is the

## Mozart in Prague

'My Praguers understand me,' once declared Mozart, who was far better received here than in Vienna. Both *Figaro* and *Don Giovanni* were hits in Prague, and after the composer's death in Vienna, it was Prague that honoured him with a great funeral mass in Malá Strana's St Nicholas' Church, attended by a crowd of 4,000 mourners.

## Josef Kajetán Tyl

The Estates Theatre (Stavovské divadlo; ➤ 75) reverted to its original name in 1991. For many years it was called the Tyl Theatre; almost unknown abroad, the 19th-century playwright Josef Kajetán Tyl is dear to Czech hearts for his comedy *Fidlovačka*, which contains the song *Kde domov můj?* ('Where is my home?'), a plaintive call that later formed the first line of the Czechoslovak national anthem.

home of the Czech Philharmonic Orchestra, which performs in the big Dvořák Hall. The Little (or Suk) Hall is used for chamber concerts.

✚ E4 ✉ Alšovo nábřeží 12, Staré město ☎ 24 89 33 52 🚇 Staroměstská

### ST AGNES'S CONVENT (ANEŽSKÝ KLÁŠTER)

One of the convent's two churches is used for chamber concerts.
➤ 41

### ST GEORGE'S BASILICA (BAZILIKA SVATÉHO JIŘÍ)

Prague Castle's austere Romanesque church is now used as a chamber concert hall.
➤ 31

### ST JAMES'S CHURCH (KOSTEL SVATÉHO JAKUBA)

The admirable acoustics in this superb Old Town church augment concerts of sacred music held here.
➤ 55

### ST NICHOLAS'S CHURCH (CHRÁM SVATÉHO MIKULÁŠE), MALÁ STRANA

The organ that Mozart played in Prague's greatest baroque church still accompanies choral concerts.
➤ 33

### ST NICHOLAS'S CHURCH, OLD TOWN (KOSTEL SVATÉHO MIKULÁŠE, STARÉ MĚSTO)

The other Church of St Nicholas, less sumptuous

than the one in Malá Strana but an equally fine venue for organ and vocal recitals.
➤ 55

### SMETANA HALL (SMETANOVA SÍŇ)

Part of the sumptuously decorated and recently renovated Municipal House, and home of the Czech Symphony Orchestra.
➤ 57

### TROJA CHÂTEAU (TROJSKÝ ZÁMEK)

The magnificence of Count Šternberg's out-of-town palace almost overwhelms the music.
➤ 48

### VILA AMERIKA

Count Michna's jolly little 18th-century summer palace, home of the Dvořák Museum, puts on evening evocations of the composer's life and work.
➤ 57

### WALLENSTEIN PALACE (VALDŠTJENSKÝ PALÁC)

Summer evening concerts in the baroque gardens of the palace are a dream.
➤ 34

# CINEMA & THEATRE

## CINEMA

Prague has dozens of cinemas, with a particular concentration around Wenceslas Square. Many show recent releases, often in the original version with Czech subtitles.

## THEATRE

The language barrier can limit enjoyment of the theatre for visitors who don't speak Czech. However, you don't have to know the language to enjoy mime and multi-media (known locally as 'Black Light' theatre), both big on the Prague stage. Most such shows are devised with the foreign visitor in mind.

### ARCHA THEATRE
Has a varied programme, much of it designed to appeal to the visitor from abroad.
✚ F4  ✉ Na poříčí 26, north Nové město  ☎ 232 75 70
🚇 Náměstí Republiky

### CELETNÁ THEATRE
One of the establishments whose shows are designed for the needs of summer visitors eager to hear more about the life and times of Prague's literary giant, Franz Kafka.
✚ E4  ✉ Celetná 17, Staré město  ☎ 24 81 27 62
🚇 Náměstí Republiky

### IMAGE THEATRE (DIVADLO IMAGE)
This is another of Prague's visitor-oriented theatres, whose 'Black Light' shows feature dance, mime, music...you name it!
✚ E4  ✉ Pařížská 4, Staré město  ☎ 232 91 91
🚇 Staroměstská

### JIŘÍ SRNEC BLACK THEATRE
Legends of magic Prague presented in multi-media format as at the Image Theatre.
✚ E5  ✉ Lucerna, Štěpánská 61, Nové město  ☎ 9004 9434
🚇 Národní třída

### KARLÍN MUSICAL THEATRE (HUDEBNÍ DIVADLO V KARLÍNĚ)
Operettas and musicals are the undemanding fare in this inner-suburban theatre.
✚ F4  ✉ Křižíkova 10, Karlín  ☎ 2186 8149
🚇 Florenc

### LATERNA MAGIKA
The Magic Lantern's synthesis of film, music, theatre and mime was first developed in the 1950s by Alfréd Radok, and continues to intrigue and delight audiences. Some of the most successful shows are reworkings of ancient myths, such as Theseus and the Minotaur or the *Odyssey*.
✚ D/E5  ✉ Nová scéna of the National Theatre, Národní třída 2, Nové město  ☎ 24 91 41 29
🚇 Národní třída

### NATIONAL THEATRE (NÁRODNÍ DIVADLO)
You can see classics of Czech theatre here, as well as performances of opera and ballet.
✚ D/E5  ✉ Národní třída 2, Nové město  ☎ 24 91 34 37
🚇 Národní třída

## Keeping you posted
Since 1989 there has been a boom in performances of all kinds intended to appeal to foreign visitors. Posters and leaflets will keep you up to date with what's on, as well as the English-language *Prague Post* weekly newspaper.

## Czech puppetry

In a country where the art of manipulating marionettes can be studied at university, no one whose imagination has been stimulated by the array of delightful little figures on sale on stalls and in shops should miss one of Prague's puppet performances. The colourful characters are mostly drawn from the fairy-tales that are such a feature of Czech popular literature. They include water sprites and witches, devils, soldiers and highwaymen, villains and virgins.

### ROKOKO

Some non-Czech performances are put on in this establishment. In Wenceslas Square.

🕂 E5 ✉ Václavské náměstí 38, Nové město ☎ 24 21 71 13 🚇 Můstek

### TA FANTASTIKA

Another spectacle based on the Black Light fusion of dance, mime and music – a spin-off from the hugely successful Laterna Magika.

🕂 E4 ✉ Karlova 8, Staré město ☎ 2423 7763 🚇 Staroměstská

### THEATRE ON THE BALUSTRADE (DIVADLO NA ZÁBRADLÍ)

Václav Havel shifted scenery here and his later plays helped build the theatre's reputation.

🕂 E4 ✉ Anenské náměstí 5, Staré město ☎ 24 22 95 17. Box office: 24 22 19 33 or 24 22 95 17 🚇 Staroměstská

## PUPPETRY & FOLKLORE

### CZECH FOLKLORE ENSEMBLE (ČESKÝ SOUBOR PÍSNÍ A TANCŮ)

Well-rehearsed rustic song and dance, plus some operettas.

🕂 D4 ✉ Divadlo na Klárově (Klarov Theatre), nábřeží E Beneše 3, Malá Strana ☎ 53 98 37 🚇 Malostranská

### DIVADLO MIMŮ

Pantomime in the suburbs.

🕂 F3 ✉ Františka křížka 36, Holešovice ☎ 2057 1584 🚊 Tram 5, 12, 17

### MINOR THEATRE (DIVADLO MINOR)

Live theatre for children, as well as puppetry, in continuous performances.

🕂 F4 ✉ Senovážné náměstí 28, Nové město ☎ 2422 9675 🚇 Náměstí Republiky

### NATIONAL MARIONETTE THEATRE (NÁRODNÍ DIVADLO MARIONET)

Adaptations of operas feature among other attractions. Matinée performances.

🕂 E4 ✉ Žatecká 1, Staré město ☎ 232 34 29 🚇 Staroměstská

### SPEJBL AND HURVÍNEK THEATRE (DIVADLO SPEJBLA A HURVÍNKA)

Don't miss the antics of Prague's immortal puppet duo: Josef Skupa's troubled father and his perky son have been performing in their own theatre since 1945.

🕂 C3 ✉ Dejvická 38 ☎ 2431 6784 🚇 Dejvická

# SPORT & OUTDOOR ACTIVITIES

## FOOTBALL

### SPARTA STADIUM

First-class football at the home of the country's leading club, Sparta.

➕ E3 ✉ Milady Horákové 98, Letná ☎ 2057 0328 🚋 Tram 26 to Sparta

## ICE HOCKEY

### SPARTA PRAHA

This big indoor hall is the base of HC Sparta Praha.

➕ F2 ✉ Výstaviště (Exhibition Grounds), Holešovice ☎ 872 7477 🚇 Holešovice

## SKATING

### SPORTS HALL

This indoor ice-rink is one of several in Prague. In winter there's also skating on ponds, lakes and reservoirs on the outskirts of the city.

➕ F2 ✉ Exhibition Grounds (Výstaviště), Holešovice ☎ 37 11 42 🚇 Nádraží Holešovice 🚋 Tram 5, 12, 17 to Výstaviště

## SWIMMING

### HOSTIVAŘ RESERVOIR

Prague's biggest reservoir; there are windsurfing and boating opportunities, as well as swimming.

➕ Off map, 12km south-east of Prague 🚇 Háje, then walk or Bus 165, 170, 212, 213

### PODOLÍ POOLS (PLAVECKÝ STADION PODOLÍ)

Large complex of pools, sauna, etc.

➕ E8 ✉ Podolská 74, Podolí ☎ 61 21 43 43 🚋 Tram 3, 17 to Kublov

### SLAPY DAM & LAKE

The Vltava upstream from Prague has been dammed to form a chain of lakes. Facilities include beaches of imported sand.

➕ Off map, 30km south of Prague 🚌 Bus from Anděl bus station

## CYCLING

### LANDA

One of the few places to hire bikes.

➕ G5 ✉ Šumavská 33, Vinohrady ☎ 2425 6121 🚇 Náměstí Míru 🚋 Tram 16 to Šumavská

## HORSE-RACING

### CHUCHLE RACECOURSE (ZÁVODIŠTĚ CHUCHLE)

Flat races and trotting.

➕ Off map, 10km south of Prague ☎ 54 30 91, 54 04 06 or 54 66 10 🚂 Suburban train from Smíchov to Velká Chuchle 🚌 Bus 172

## GOLF

### KARLŠTEJN

One of a number of newish courses; this one has the benefit of Karlštejn Castle (➤ 20) as part of the scenery.

➕ Off map, 30km to the south-west ☎ 0204 67 27 27

### ŠTIŘÍN CHÂTEAU (ZÁMEK ŠTIŘÍN)

This impeccably restored country house hotel has a golf course in its park.

➕ Off map, 30km to the south-east ☎ 0311 68 47 16

### In-town cycling

Cycling is not particularly popular in this fume- and cobble-ridden city. At the weekends urban cyclists congregate in the city's extensive Stromovka Park (➕ E2), where there is a network of marked cycleways and some signposting indicating how bikers might reach other parts of Prague in relative safety.

# HOTELS BY DISTRICT

## Prices

Expect to pay per night for a double room:

£££  Kč4,500 +
££   Kč2,000–4,500
£    Kč1,000–2,000

## Book ahead

Until recently Prague suffered from an acute shortage of hotel accommodation, particularly in the middle price range, and was not a cheap place to stay. The situation has improved, but it is always wise to book well in advance, especially in summer and if you want to stay in the centre.

## HRADČANY & LESSER TOWN (MALÁ STRANA)

The Castle quarter and the 'Lesser Town' between Prague Castle and the River Vltava.

### DIPLOMAT (££–£££)

Large, immaculate, modern hotel, not quite in Hradčany but only 10 minutes (uphill) on foot from the Castle. A business person's favourite, with conference facilities, conveniently located on the run-in from the airport and next door to a Metro station a mere three stops from the city centre.
⊞ C3 ✉ Evropská 15, Dejvice ☎ 24 39 41 11 Ⓜ Dejvická

### HOFFMEISTER (£££)

In an historic building which has been carefully refurbished, 'Prague's personal luxury hotel' enjoys an enviable position below the bend in the road up to Prague Castle.
⊞ D3 ✉ Pod bruskou 7 ☎ 56 18 15 5-7 Ⓜ Malostranská

### KAMPA (££)

In a delightful corner of the Lesser Town close to the Devil's Brook, this old building has been refurbished and is popular with tour groups.
⊞ D4/5 ✉ Všehrdova 16 ☎ 5732 0404 🚊 Tram 12, 22 to Hellichova

### PENSION DIENTZENHOFER (££)

In a secluded side street, this former home of the Dientzenhofers, the

greatest of Prague's baroque architects, is now a small hotel.
⊞ D4 ✉ Nosticova 2 ☎ 53 16 72 🚊 Tram 12, 22 to Malostranské náměstí

### SAVOY (£££)

Top-of-the-market luxury within easy (downhill) reach of Prague Castle in a completely modernised hotel.
⊞ C4 ✉ Keplerova 6 ☎ 2430 2430 🚊 Tram 22 to Pohořelec

### SAX (££)

There's no closer place to Prague Castle than this little hotel just off Nerudova Street.
⊞ C4 ✉ Janský vršek 3 ☎ 53 84 22 or 53 84 98 🚊 Tram 12, 22 to Malostranské náměstí

### U PÁVA (££)

'The Peacock' preens itself on its perfect location by the Vojan Gardens in lower Malá Strana, a few short steps from Charles Bridge.
⊞ D4 ✉ U lužického semináře 32 ☎ 5732 0743 Ⓜ Malostranská

### U RAKA PENSION (£££)

Idyllically located among the stuccoed houses of Nový Svět is this extremely comfortable, rather exclusive small pension.
⊞ C3 ✉ Černínská 10 ☎ 2051 1100 🚊 Tram 22 to Brusnice

### U TŘÍ PŠTROSŮ (£££)

'The Three Ostriches' was once the centre of a flourishing trade in feathers, then a coffee-house. The exquisite gabled Renaissance building is now a rather expensive private hotel, from some of whose rooms you can almost exchange a handshake with people passing by on Charles Bridge.

➕ D4 ✉ Dražického náměstí 12 ☎ 5732 0565 🚋 Tram 12, 22 to Malostranské náměstí

## OLD TOWN (STARÉ MĚSTO)

The Old Town is linked to the Lesser Town by the superb Gothic Charles Bridge. From the eastern end of the bridge a warren of streets gives a good idea of what medieval Prague was like, and the Royal Way leads through the centre to the Old Town Square.

### BETLEM CLUB (£–££)

Small hotel offering central accommodation in the same square as Jan Hus's historic Bethlehem Chapel.

➕ E4 ✉ Betlémské náměstí 9 ☎ 24 21 68 72 🚇 Národní třída

### CENTRAL (£–££)

Somewhat run-down but quite adequate accommodation in a convenient position behind the Municipal House.

➕ E4 ✉ Rybná 8 ☎ 24 81 20 41 or 24 81 27 34 🚇 Náměstí Republiky

### CLOISTER INN (£)

Basic accommodation in what was part of State Security's malevolent empire.

➕ E4/5 ✉ Bartolomějská 9 ☎ 232 12 89 🚇 Národní třída

### INTERCONTINENTAL (£££)

The epitome of pretension in Communist days and hypermodern when it opened back in the 1970s, the Intercontinental offers every comfort as well as spacious public rooms furnished with fine antiques.

➕ E4 ✉ Náměstí Curieových 5 ☎ 24 88 11 11 🚇 Staroměstská

### PAŘÍŽ (£££)

The rampant early-1900s splendour of the 'Paris' has recently been restored to perfection.

➕ E4 ✉ U Obecního domu 1 ☎ 24 22 21 51 🚇 Náměstí Republiky

### U KRÁLE JIŘÍHO (£)

A small hotel just off the Royal Way with comfortable rooms and the dubious bonus of a pub on the ground floor.

➕ E4 ✉ Liliová 10 ☎ 24 22 20 13 🚇 Staroměstská

### UNGELT (£££)

Apartment hotel in ancient premises that once formed part of the city's customs house.

➕ E4 ✉ Štupartská 1 ☎ 24 81 13 30 🚇 Náměstí Republiky

## NEW TOWN (NOVÉ MĚSTO) AND NEAR BY

'New' in the 14th century, but developed in the late

## Special offers

The number of moderately priced hotels has increased rapidly, but they are probably still outnumbered by expensive hotels. However, it's always worth checking to see if the latter are offering any special deals, particularly for weekend stays.

## Breathe freely

Choosing a place to stay requires care. A central location may turn out to be noisy with traffic as the rush hour gets under way shortly after 5AM. Somewhere in the suburbs may seem a long way from the action, but if the hotel is near a Metro station this is unlikely to be a problem and your night's rest may be more relaxed because you are breathing air that is fresher (albeit marginally so).

19th and early 20th centuries, this part of Prague centres on Wenceslas Square and the broad streets of Narodní and Na příkopě

### ADRIA (£££)
A stunningly restored old establishment amid the glitter of Wenceslas Square.
✚ E5 ✉ Václavské náměstí 26 ☎ 24 21 65 43 or 24 23 13 80 Ⓜ Můstek

### AMETYST (££–£££)
A fresh and inviting medium-sized, family-owned hotel, the equal in luxury to most of the big names and only 10 minutes' walk from Wenceslas Square.
✚ F6 ✉ Jana Masaryka 11, Vinohrady ☎ 2425 4185 Ⓜ Náměstí Míru

### ANNA (£–££)
A reliable small hotel in the pleasant inner suburb of Vinohrady, less than a quarter of an hour's stroll from Wenceslas Square.
✚ G5 ✉ Budečská 17, Vinohrady ☎ 25 41 63 Ⓜ Náměstí Míru

### ATLANTIK (££)
A pleasant alternative to the Harmony (see below) if you want to stay on this busy central shopping street close to the city centre.
✚ F4 ✉ Na poříčí 9 ☎ 24 81 10 84 Ⓜ Náměstí Republiky

### ATRIUM (£££)
Around the vast interior space which gives this hotel its name are nearly 800 beds, just enough to accommodate the US

president's entourage when he came to Prague.
✚ F3 ✉ Pobřežní 1 ☎ 24 84 11 11 Ⓜ Florenc

### BILÁ LABUT (££)
A moderately priced hotel, run by the Best Western chain.
✚ F4 ✉ Biskupská 9, Nové město ☎ 2481 1382 Ⓜ Náměstí Republiky

### CITY HOTEL MORÁŇ (£££)
Austrian-style elegance and comfort in an historic building close to Charles Square.
✚ E6 ✉ Na Moráni 15 ☎ 24 91 52 08 Ⓜ Karlovo náměstí

### CITY PENSION (£)
Exceptionally pleasant pension, one Metro stop from Wenceslas Square.
✚ F6 ✉ Belgická 10 ☎ 691 13 34 Ⓜ Náměstí Míru

### EVROPA (£–££)
Nothing could be closer to Prague's heart than this art-nouveau jewel on Wenceslas Square. Unfortunately, most of the rooms fail to live up to the promise of the exterior.
✚ E5 ✉ Václavské náměstí 25 ☎ 24 22 81 17 Ⓜ Můstek

### HARMONY (££)
A 1930s building just east of the Municipal House which has been attractively refurbished to provide pleasant accommodation.
✚ F4 ✉ Na poříčí 31 ☎ 23 20 016 Ⓜ Náměstí Republiky

### HOTEL 16 U SV KATEŘINY (£–££)
Excellent-value family hotel just around the

corner from the Dvořák Museum and a 10-minute walk from Wenceslas Square.

➕ E5 ✉ Kateřinská 16
☎ 29 53 29 or 29 13 13
Ⓜ I P Pavlova

## JALTA (£££)

The air-conditioned Jalta is a fine example of 1950s architecture, and has an unbeatable location towards the top of Wenceslas Square.

➕ F5 ✉ Václavské náměstí 45, Nové město ☎ 2422 9133
Ⓜ Muzeum or Můstek

## PALACE (£££)

A sumptuous art-nouveau exterior conceals the completely refurbished ultramodern interior of the Palace, proud to be Prague's priciest hotel.

➕ E4 ✉ Panská 12
☎ 24 09 31 11 Ⓜ Můstek

## PÁV (££)

Family-run pension in a side street that also happens to be the location of Prague's most popular beer hall.

➕ E5 ✉ Křemencova 13
☎ 24 91 32 86 Ⓜ Národní třída

## THE SUBURBS

Beyond the four historic districts is a ring of suburbs, some dull, but most with their own attractions.

## BILÝ LEV (££)

An economical place in the eastern suburb of Žižkov to rest your bones.

➕ G4 ✉ Cimburkova 20
☎ 27 11 26 🚋 Trams 5, 9, 26 to Husinecká

## COUBERTIN (£)

Small modern hotel named after the founder of the modern Olympics, and located among the stadia and sports facilities of Strahov.

➕ B5 ✉ Atletická 4, Strahov
☎ 35 28 51 Ⓜ Dejvická, then Bus 149, 217

## FORUM (£££)

International luxury and all that that implies in a steel and glass tower overlooking the Nusle expressway bridge in Vyšehrad. Wenceslas Square is just five minutes away by Metro.

➕ F7 ✉ Kongresová 1, Vyšehrad ☎ 61 19 11 11
Ⓜ Vyšehrad

## GOLF (£)

Large motel handily located on the main run-in from the west.

➕ Off map to west of Prague ✉ Plzeňská 215
☎ 52 32 51

## HOLIDAY INN PRAGUE (£££)

This unique and long-established hotel (previously the International) in a Socialist-Realist skyscraper retains all the atmosphere of the Stalinist 1950s.

➕ C2 ✉ Koulova 15
☎ 24 39 31 11 Ⓜ Dejvická
🚋 Tram 20, 25 to Podbaba

## KAFKA (£)

Good-value accommodation on the wrong side of the tracks in the seedy inner suburb of Žižkov, but only 10 minutes' walk from the main railway station and

## Botels

An alternative to conventional hotels are the 'botels' moored along the banks of the Vltava at various points. However, being rather cramped, they are less romantic than they might sound. One such, close to the Palacký Bridge (Palackého most) on the Smíchov quayside, is the Admirál (➤ 77).

## Home from home

An economical solution to the accommodation problem is to stay in a private house or, more likely, a flat. Most agencies have such places on their books, which is a better approach than allowing yourself to be solicited as you stand around helplessly on arrival at the main railway station. Private rooms can also be booked from abroad, for example through the Czechbook Agency (✉ St John's Park, Blackheath, London SE3 7JP, England ☎ 0181 853 1168). Check that it doesn't take three changes of bus and tram to get into town from your accommodation.

a short tram ride to Wenceslas Square.
✚ G4 ✉ Cimburkova 24 ☎ 27 31 01 🚊 Tram 5, 9, 26 to Husinecká

### LOUDA (£)

Pleasant pension usefully located on a residential road running off the main highway to northern Bohemia and eastern Germany.
✚ H1 ✉ Kubišova 10 ☎ 688 14 91

### OBORA (££)

Well-appointed small hotel in the leafy surroundings of the royal hunting park and Hvězda Castle, in the western outskirts close to the airport.
✚ Off map to west of Prague ✉ Libocká 271/1 ☎ 36 77 79

### PRAHA (£££)

The Praha expresses perfectly how Communist taste had moved on from the Stalinist certainties of the International Hotel of the 1950s (► 85; now the Holiday Inn) to the anonymous luxury of the 1970s. Until 1989 the Praha, in its hill-top location in the western suburb of Dejvice, was reserved for privileged and powerful Party people and their guests.
✚ B2 ✉ Sušická 20, Dejvice ☎ 2434 1111 🚇 Dejvická 🚊 Tram 2, 20, 26 to Hadovka

### VILA VOYTA (£££)

This splendid Secession villa in the southern suburbs caters for its mostly business clientele

with great care and attention.
✚ Off map to south of Prague ✉ K novému dvoru 124/54, Lhotka ☎ 472 27 60

## ACCOMMODATION ADVICE

Any number of agencies stand ready to help you with advice on accommodation.

AVE is one of the best established, with offices at the airport, the main railway station (✉ Hlavní nádraží, Wilsonova 8 ☎ 24 22 35 21) and Holešovice railway station. Prague Information Service (Pražská informační služba – PIS ☎ 2448 2202), the official city information agency, will also find lodgings. They have offices at the main railway station, Old Town Square and Na příkopě (► 19).

# PRAGUE
## *travel facts*

# ARRIVING & DEPARTING

## Before you go
- Visas are not required for citizens of the UK, USA, Canada and most European countries.

## When to go
- The best times to visit are in spring, when the fruit trees of Petřín Hill are in blossom, and in early summer.
- Winter weather can be depressingly grey and cold, with high levels of air pollution.
- High summer can become oppressively hot and humid, with considerable rainfall.

## Arriving by air
- There are direct flights to Ruzyně Airport from most major European cities, as well as from New York and Montréal.
- Prague is served by ČSA (the national airline), as well as by other major carriers.
- The best city-centre link is by airport bus, either to Dejvická Metro station or to Náměstí Republiky on the eastern edge of the Old Town. An ordinary city bus is marginally cheaper but meanders all over the suburbs. For taxis, ➤ 91.
- The ČSA main office is at ✉ V celnici 5, Staré město ☎ 2010 4111.

## Arriving by train
- Express trains link Prague to all neighbouring countries, as well as to Paris and to Ostend in Belgium (ferry connection with Dover in England).
- Most trains terminate at the main station (Hlavní nádraží), though some call (or terminate) at Holešovice in the northern suburbs or at Smíchov in the southern suburbs, both of which have good onward connections by Metro.
- Czech Railways (ČD) has an information office at the north end of level 3 in the main railway station ✉ 2422 4200.

## Arriving by car
- Good main roads link Prague to all neighbouring countries, and the motorway linking it with Plžen (Pilsen) and the border with Bavaria is almost complete. Prague is less than 1,100km from Calais, with its frequent ferry services to Dover as well as the Channel Tunnel Shuttle. The best Channel crossing is the Dover–Ostend SeaCat service (2 hours).

## Arriving by coach
- Express coaches link Prague with a growing number of international destinations, including London.
- The coach terminakis at Florenc, to the east of the city centre, where there is a Metro station.
- Departure tickets can be obtained at Florenc, but it is easier to buy them through a travel agency.

## Arriving by boat
- Occasional passenger boats ply the Vltava and Elbe to Dresden and on to Hamburg.

## Customs regulations
- The duty-free allowance comprises 200 cigarettes or 100 cigars or 250g tobacco; 2 litres of wine; 1 litre of spirits; 50ml perfume and 250ml *eau de toilette*.
- There is no limit on the import or export of foreign currencies.
- In principle, there are strict limits on the export of goods purchased in the country, but normal tourist souvenirs are unlikely to pose

any problem. However, antiques and 'rare cultural objects' require an official certificate from a recognised museum or art gallery (which the dealer may already have obtained).

# ESSENTIAL FACTS

## Travel insurance
- All visitors should have full travel insurance.
- UK citizens may enjoy free medical treatment in an emergency, but taking out medical insurance ensures rapid repatriation and can help in cutting through bureaucracy.

## Opening hours
- Banks: normally Mon–Fri 9–5. Komerční banka ✉ Na příkopě 3 is open Mon–Fri 8–5, and Česká spořitelna ✉ Vádavské náměsti 16 is open Mon–Fri 8–6.
- Shops: Mon–Fri 9–6; Sat 9–1. Food stores may open as early as 7AM; there is some late-night shopping (to 8PM) on Thu. Some shops in tourist areas also open on Sun.
- Museums and galleries: Tue–Sun 9/10–5. They close Mon, except the National Museum (open Mon and closed Tue) and the Strahov Library (open every day). Some also close for lunch.

## National holidays
- 1 January, Easter Monday, 1 May (Labour Day), 8 May (Liberation Day), 5 July (SS Cyril and Methodius), 6 July (Jan Hus's Day), 28 October (Independence Day), 24–6 December.

## Money matters
- The Czech crown (*koruna česká* or Kč) is divided into 100 virtually worthless hellers (*halér*).

- There are coins for 10, 20 and 50 hellers, and for 1, 2, 5, 10, 20 and 50 crowns, and notes in denominations of 20, 50, 100, 200, 500, 1,000, 2,000 and 5,000 crowns.
- There are plenty of *bureaux de change*, but banks usually give better rates of exchange.
- Credit cards are in increasing use, particularly in places frequented by tourists.

## Etiquette
- Czech manners tend to be formal. Titles such as Doctor and Professor must not be ignored, and hands should be shaken when offered.
- Dress, however, is less formal; neat casual wear is usually acceptable, though attendance at the opera requires a modicum of formality.
- Diners share tables in crowded restaurants, and exchange greetings such as '*dobrý den*' ('good day'), '*dobrou chuť*' ('enjoy your meal'), '*na zdraví!*' ('cheers!') and '*na shledanou*' ('goodbye') at the appropriate moments.
- If invited into a Czech home, take flowers or a small gift, and offer to take your shoes off before entering.

## Women travellers
- Women travellers need take no more than the usual precautions when visiting Prague.
- Unaccompanied females lingering at night in certain areas of the city – such as parts of Wenceslas Square – may be taken for prostitutes.

## Places of worship
- Anglican: St Clement's Church (sv Klimenta) ✉ Klimentská, north Nové

město 🅿 Náměstí Republiky 🕐 English-
language service Sun 11AM.

- Roman Catholic: St Joseph's
Church (sv Josefa) ✉ Josefská 4, Malá
Strana 🅿 Malostranská 🕐 English mass Sun
10:30AM.

## Student travellers

- Few discounts are available for
students, but by keeping out of
the most popular tourist spots,
young people will find it a cheap
city to get by in.
- All aspects of youth travel and
accommodation are dealt with by
the ČKM agency ✉ Jindřišská 28,
Nové město ☎ 26 85 32 🅿 Můstek or
Náměstí Republiky

## Time differences

- Central European Time (GMT
plus an hour) applies, changed
for daylight saving between
March and September.

## Toilets

- 'WC', 'OO', *muži/páni* (Gents) and
*ženy/dámy* (Ladies) are useful
signs to remember.
- Public facilities are rare; look for
those in restaurants, cafés, etc.
- Tip the attendant (usually an old
woman) with some smaller coins –
these are her wages.

## Electricity

- 230 volts, 50 cycles AC, fed
through standard continental
two-pin plugs.

## PUBLIC TRANSPORT

- Prague's comprehensive transport
system is based on the immaculate underground Metro and the
slightly less pristine but equally
reliable trams and buses.
- One cheap ticket obtained at
stations, kiosks and some hotel
receptions serves all three

modes and must be validated
by inserting it into the clipping
machine as you enter a station
or board a vehicle. A fresh ticket
must be used for each change
of mode.

- The best public transport plan is
in the city guide available from
the Prague Information Service
(► 19). This shows all Metro and
tram lines and, very usefully,
names tram stops and Metro
stations.
- Expect crowding during rush
hours (although they start and
finish earlier than in many
Western countries). The young
and fit should give up their seats
to the elderly, pregnant women
and those with disabilities.

## Metro

- This showpiece system, with its
fast and frequent trains and clean
stations, consists of three lines:
A (colour-coded green), B
(yellow) and C (red). They
converge from the suburbs on
the city centre where there are
several interchange stations.
- To ensure you get on the right
train, check the line (A, B or C)
and note the name of the
terminus station at the end of
the line in the direction you wish
to travel; this station appears on
the overhead direction signs.
- Outlying stations are relatively far
apart and are intended more to
feed commuters to connecting
trams and buses than to take
tourists to their favourite spots.
- Particularly useful stations are
Můstek (for Wenceslas Square
and Old Town Square),
Staroměstská (for Old Town
Square) and Malostranská (for
Malá Strana and for Tram No 22).
Hradčanská station is quite a
long walk from Prague Castle.

## Tram

- The tramway system operates in close conjunction with its underground equivalent. It is worth while studying the route map, as travel by tram can spare your legs on many of your likely itineraries.
- The name of every tram stop appears on the stop sign and on the route map.
- Tram routes are numbered and the tram has a destination board. Timetables are usually pasted on the stop and are almost always adhered to.
- There is a skeleton service of night trams with a system of numbers and schedules that differs from the daytime service.
- A particularly useful and scenic line is the No 22, which runs from downtown (at Národní třída) right through Malá Strana, past Malostranská Metro station, then climbs to the back entrance of Prague Castle (Pražský hrad stop) or continues to Strahov Monastery.

## Bus

- Kept out of the city centre to minimise pollution, buses serve all the suburban parts which the trams cannot reach.

## Discounts

- Special passes are valid for periods of one day upwards. They are useful only if you intend to make lots of trips – more than about eight a day.

## Taxi

- Prague taxi-drivers have an appalling reputation for their overcharging and for their disagreeable nature.
- If you have to use a taxi, agree the fare beforehand. Asking for a receipt can be helpful in reducing excessive demands.
- It may be better to flag down a moving taxi rather than go to a taxi rank.
- For taxis, telephone AAA Radiotaxi ☎ 1080 or Profitaxi ☎ 1035
- The smarter hotels have their own taxi service, reliable but expensive.

# MEDIA & COMMUNICATIONS

## Telephones

- The Czech Republic's phone system is being modernised, and making calls can be very frustrating. All Prague subscribers have been, or are being, allotted new numbers.
- Most public phones now take phone cards, on sale in kiosks and post offices in denominations of Kč150 upwards.
- Note that telephoning from your hotel may cost up to four times the standard rate.

## Mail

- Postage stamps can be bought not only at post offices but also at kiosks and hotel receptions.
- The main post office, with fax and poste restante services, is at ✉ Jindřišská 14, Nové město ☎ 24 22 88 56 Ⓜ Můstek.

## Newspapers and magazines

- Foreign-language newspapers are on sale at city centre news-stands and at some hotel receptions.
- The leading English-language publication is the weekly *Prague Post*, with useful listings.
- The English-language *Central European Business Weekly* is much as its title suggests.

91

- The German-language weekly *Prager Zeitung* is oriented towards the minuscule German population still living in the Czech Republic.

### Radio and television

- Local TV consists of four channels – ČT1 and ČT2 (state owned), and Nova and Prima (private) – none of which is likely to be of much interest to those who don't speak Czech. Major hotels have multiple satellite channels.
- Local Radio 1 (91.9 FM) puts out news of tourist interest in English at 3:30PM on weekdays.
- BBC World Service and Voice of America can be picked up on 101.0 FM and 1197kHz MW respectively.
- Most local stations play rock's 'golden oldies'. Country Radio (89.5 FM) plays country music; Radio 1 (91.9 FM) plays avant-garde rock; and Classic FM (98.7 FM) plays classical music.

## EMERGENCIES

### Sensible precautions

- Despite some horror stories, Prague is still safer than most comparable Western cities.
- The main hazard is the pickpockets who operate in tourist areas – on Wenceslas Square, on Charles Bridge and in Old Town Square. Keep a good hold on your handbag and don't walk around with your wallet protruding from a back pocket.
- A common scam is for someone to accost you with an innocent-seeming enquiry about money or the location of the nearest bank. His 'policeman' accomplice will then appear and relieve you of your passport if you are unwise enough to produce it.

### Lost property

- The lost property office is at ✉ Karoliny Světlé 5, Staré město ☎ 24 23 50 85.

### Medical treatment

- Emergency medical treatment is done under contract in Prague so it is advisable to arrange medical insurance in advance of your trip.
- Foreigners' Polyclinic ✉ Roentgenova 2, Motol (off map) ☎ 52 92 21 46 🚊 Tram 4, 7, 9, 58, or Bus 167 from Anděl Metro. Bring your passport to this former Communist Party clinic, which forms part of the Nemocnice, Na Homolce, the huge hospital complex just off the main highway to Pilsen in the western suburb of Motol. It is the best place to go for serious treatment.
- Fakultní poliklinika ✚ E5 ✉ Karlovo náměstí 32, Nové město ☎ 2490 4111 🚇 Karlovo náměstí. A downtown alternative to the above for less serious ailments.
- Drugs and medicaments must be paid for. Remember to bring supplies of any regular medication with you.
- Pharmacies that stay open 24 hours a day can be found at ✉ Palackého 5 and ✉ Bergická 27.

### Emergency phone numbers

- Ambulance ☎ 155.
- Police ☎ 158.
- Fire brigade ☎ 150.

### Embassies

- Canada: ✚ D3 ✉ Mickiewiczova 6, Hradčany ☎ 24 31 11 08 🚇 Hradčany.
- United Kingdom: ✚ D4 ✉ Thunovská 14, Malá Strana ☎ 5732 0663 🚇 Malostranská, then Tram 12, 22.
- USA: ✚ D4 ✉ Tržiště 15, Malá Strana ☎ 5732 0355 🚇 Malostranská, then Tram 12, 22.

# LANGUAGE

- Czech is a Slavonic language, so anyone who knows other Slav languages such as Russian or Polish should have little difficulty in muddling through.
- It will be rewarding to master a few words and phrases, if only to be able to ask if anyone speaks your language and to recognise some signs.
- Czech is pronounced as it is written (unlike English).

## Vowels

a  as in mammoth  á as in father
é  as in air       e  as in yes
i,y as in city      í,ý as in meet
o  as in top        ó as in more
u  as in book       ů as in boom

## Consonants

c  as in its        č as in china
ch as in Scottish loch
j  as in yes        n as in onion
r  rolled or trilled r  ř combination
                       of r and z (as
                       in Dvořák)
š  as in shine
z  as in zero       ž as in pleasure

## Basic words and phrases

yes ano
no ne
please prosím
thank you děkuji
do you speak  English/German?
   mluvíte anglicky /německy?
I don't understand nerozumím
I don't speak Czech nemluvím česky
hello ahoj
good morning/good day dobrý den
goodnight dobrou noc
goodbye na shledanou
sorry promiňte
where? kde?
how much? kolik?
when? kdy?
what? co?

## Numbers

| | | | |
|---|---|---|---|
| 1 | jeden/jedna/jedno | 15 | patnáct/ |
| 2 | dva/dvě | 16 | šestnáct |
| 3 | tři | 17 | sedmnáct |
| 4 | čtyři | 18 | osmnáct |
| 5 | pět | 19 | devatenáct |
| 6 | šest | 20 | dvacet |
| 7 | sedm | 30 | třicet |
| 8 | osm | 40 | čtyřicet |
| 9 | devět | 50 | padesát |
| 10 | deset | 60 | šedesát |
| 11 | jedenáct | 70 | sedmdesát |
| 12 | dvanáct | 80 | osmdesát |
| 13 | třináct | 90 | devadesát |
| 14 | čtrnáct | 100 | sto |
| | | 1,000 | tisíc |

## Days of the week

Monday pondělí    Friday pátek
Tuesday úterý     Saturday sobota
Wednesday středa  Sunday neděle
Thursday čvrtek

## Months of the year

January leden      July červenec
February únor      August srpen
March březen       September září
April duben        October říjen
May květen         November listopad
June červen        December prosinec

## Useful words

beer pivo
big velký/á/é
bus or tram stop zastávka
café kavárna
castle hradhrad
closed zavřeno
Danger! pozor!
entrance vchod/vstup
exit východ/výstup
forbidden zákaz
market trh
open otevřeno
pharmacy lékarna
pull (sign on door) sem
push (sign on door) tam
small malý/á/é
station nádraží
water voda

# INDEX